The Midrash Key

Tracing Jesus' Teachings to Their Old Testament Jewish Roots

By Edward J. Vasicek

© 2010 Edward J. Vasicek

I dedicate this book to my loving wife, Marylu, who, after thirty years of marriage, is still my joy and my reward in this life. Without her support, I would have been a ministry casualty time and time again.

List of Bible Versions and Copyright Information

The Default Bible Translation Used in This Book is the New International Version.

NIV. All scripture quotations, unless otherwise indicated, are taken from the Holy Bible, New International Version®, NIV®. Copyright ©1973, 1978, 1984 by Biblica, Inc.™ Used by permission of Zondervan. All rights reserved worldwide. www.zondervan.com

Other Versions Are Cited By Abbreviation as Follows:

KJV. is the abbreviation for the *King James Version* of the Bible, public domain.

NKJV. Scripture quotations marked "NKJV™" are taken from the *New King James Version*®. Copyright © 1982 by Thomas Nelson, Inc. Used by permission. All rights reserved.

NASB. Scripture quotations taken from the *New American Standard Bible*®, Copyright © 1960, 1962, 1963, 1968, 1971, 1972, 1973, 1975, 1977, 1995 by The Lockman Foundation. Used by permission. (www.Lockman.org)

ESV. Scripture quotations marked ESV are from The Holy Bible, *English Standard Version*® (ESV®), copyright © 2001 by Crossway, a publishing ministry of Good News Publishers. Used by permission. All rights reserved.

The Midrash Key

Table of Contents...

Introduction	4
Chapter 1: Theological Backgrounds and Preliminaries: Jesus, One of Many Rabbis?	8
Chapter 2: The Problem Within	31
Chapter 3: Midrashim on the Mount, Part One: Light, Divorce, Vows	47
Chapter 4: Midrashim on the Mount, Part Two: Materialism, Riches, and God's Provision	67
Chapter 5: Midrashim on the Mount, Part Three: Lending and Perfection	90
Chapter 6: Midrashim on the Mount, Part Four: Midrashim Leviticus on the Mount	103
Chapter 7: Love for God and Others	121
Chapter 8: The Great Prophet	144
Chapter 9: Midrashim Grace and Faith	159
Chapter 10: Discipleship Midrash	181
Conclusion	198
Glossary	202
Bibliography	205

Introduction

The infusion of "Jewish Roots" material is honing our understanding of Jesus' teachings and ministry. On the one hand, some theological liberals have drawn conclusions in accord with their unbelief. On the other hand, some theological conservatives have recognized the value of these insights, but their discoveries often remain cloistered within the academic world. Except for Messianic Jews or conservative scholars who target Jewish roots studies, it seems that most academics, pastors, and laymen are left in the dark. Understanding the ancient Jewish perspective is invaluable when it comes to interpreting Jesus' words.

This "Jewish Roots" infusion is a recent phenomenon. It began as a seedling after World War II and has blossomed since that time. We will not document the historical details behind this infusion, but we can summarize them. They include: the discovery of the Dead Sea Scrolls, Jewish scholars who became interested in the teachings of Jesus from a Jewish perspective,[1] the rise of the Messianic Jewish movement, the availability of Jewish resources (like the *Talmud*) to Christians, the formation of the modern State of Israel, and a decline in Christian anti-Semitism.[2] These trickling streams have melded into a notable river.

---

[1] Particularly David Flusser and Shmuel Safrai.
[2] The rise of Dispensationalism – with its emphasis upon God's faithfulness to the Jews – not only reduced anti-Semitism, but also paved the way for Messianic Judaism.

Conservative interpreters, like myself, find that understanding Jesus' Jewish side solidifies the claim that he is the Messiah, emphasizes that his blood atoned for our sins via a penal sacrifice, and reaffirms that he is indeed "the way, the truth, and the life." [3] My hope is that the reader will gain new insight into the method and meaning of Jesus' teachings, teachings that relate to our everyday thinking and behavior. I intend this book to be the first in a series. Although it may be a stretch for some, I have worked hard to make this book understandable. Readers should feel free to refer to the glossary near the end of the book as needed.

Throughout these studies, I have experienced the overwhelming sense that I was entering into the thought process of Jesus and could envision how he planned some of his sermons. My prayer is that you, the reader, will be able to do the same. We enter holy ground together.

My contention is this: *the second-century church threw away the key to interpreting some of the nuances of Scripture* because of anti-Semitism. This key affects our interpretation of the four Gospels and passages throughout the *Second* (New) *Testament*.

Church leaders had divorced Jesus from his Jewish context and emphasized his deity to the exclusion of his humanity. They repelled Jewish believers, those most likely to understand the Jewish context of Yeshua's words. As a result, Christ's words became

---

[3] Remember, John 14:6 was delivered to a Jewish audience. Thus, there is no way to salvation other than through Jesus; even God-given Jewish religion – without Jesus – is inadequate.

more mysterious to future generations than they were to that first generation. Our goal is to increase context and return to a simpler, fuller understanding of the Savior's words. Despite the church's loss of Jewish context, the most *crucial* truths of Scriptures have always been clear. I do not want to be misunderstood: *The Midrash Key* is about nuances, not major doctrinal issues.

Let me be straightforward about my convictions. I confess my belief in the Trinity, the deity and humanity of Jesus, his virgin birth, sinless life, atoning death, physical resurrection, ascension, and promised return. I acknowledge the Bible as the verbally inspired, inerrant Word of God. It is the only infallible authority for faith and practice. In short, I acknowledge all the fundamentals of Biblical Christianity.

Although we may begin with the fundamentals, we will not end there. I will challenge the reader's hidden assumptions, assumptions that can create paradigm blindness. We will no longer merely see what we expect to see, but we will hopefully enter a fuller understanding as we interpret in light of *Midrash*.

We will briefly discuss the concept of *Midrash* in the first chapter, but regarding the use of *Midrash,* we must start somewhere. Jacob Neusner clarifies what *Midrash* could mean:

> The word "Midrash" is generally used in three senses.
>
> [1] It may refer to a compilation of scriptural exegeses, as in "the Midrash says," meaning, "the document contains the following…"

[2] It may refer to an exegesis of Scripture, as in, "this Midrash shows us…" meaning, "this interpretation of the verse at hand indicates…"

[3] It may refer to a particular mode of scripture interpretation, as in the phrase, "the Jewish Midrash holds," meaning (it is supposed) that a particular Judaic way of reading Scripture yields such-and-such results; or a particular hermeneutic identified with Judaism teaches us to read in this way rather than in some other."[4]

I do not refer to *Midrash* in the first sense, except when quoting a written *Midrash* in the footnotes. My use of *Midrash* generally incorporates elements of definitions two and three. **A *Midrash* is an Old Testament text interpreted and applied, sometimes in a sermon; it is a Jewish-style teaching based upon a text.** David Flusser writes:

> It appears that all the books of the New Testament and all those persons who were active during the period of early Christianity also had an affinity to the world of the Midrash.[5]

We are ready to begin considering a new angle by which to interpret many of Jesus' teachings: *Midrash*.

Edward J. Vasicek
The Midrash Detective

---

[4] Neusner, Jacob, *A Midrash Reader*, p. 3.
[5] Flusser, David, *Jewish Sources in Early Christianity*, p. 61

Chapter 1: Theological Backgrounds and Preliminaries: Jesus, One of Many Rabbis?

> Coming to his hometown, he began teaching the people in their synagogue, and they were amazed. "Where did this man get this wisdom and these miraculous powers?" they asked. "Isn't this the carpenter's son? Isn't his mother's name Mary, and aren't his brothers James, Joseph, Simon and Judas? Aren't all his sisters with us? Where then did this man get all these things?" And they took offense at him (Matthew 13:54-57a).

On the One Hand, Yeshua (Jesus) Was Different

> *The Incarnation*

Yeshua differed from any other rabbi who walked the earth. His conception was one of a kind. Although born normally, he was conceived supernaturally; his mother, whose Hebrew name was Miriam, was miraculously impregnated by the Holy Spirit while she was yet a biological virgin.

Eventually Mary and Joseph parented four naturally-conceived sons and a number of daughters,[6] but Jesus had the honor of being Miriam's firstborn.[7] Joseph kept Mary a virgin only until Jesus was born.[8]

Like other Jewish lads, Yeshua learned the trade of his (step) father. Joseph eked out a living in the construction trade. Our English Bibles designate him as a "carpenter," but this translation ignores the broad meaning of the Greek word; although Jesus and Joseph

---

[6] See Matthew 13:54-57 quoted at the beginning of this chapter.
[7] Luke 2:7a reads, "and she gave birth to her firstborn, a son."
[8] Matthew 1:25a states, "But he had no union with her *until* she gave birth to a son."

certainly worked with some wood, stone would have been the more common building material.[9]

Like other Jewish boys, Yeshua prepared for his *Bar Mitzvah*, meaning "Son of the Commandment." At age 13, boys experienced this Jewish rite of passage, a rite that deemed them fully responsible to obey the Torah. Devout Jews began preparing their children from infancy, talking of God's Law on a daily basis and committing it to memory.[10] The 12-year old Yeshua spent time in the temple courts, learning and questioning the rabbis who gathered for this purpose. This was typical; what was atypical was Jesus' perceptive nature, reasoning skills, and knowledge base (cf. Luke 2:47). Perhaps even the aged rabbi Hillel observed the impressive young Galilean and discussed matters with him.[11]

Theologically, God the Son became a man at the incarnation. He set aside the *use* of his special abilities as God[12] and worked no miracles until after the Holy Spirit came upon

---

[9] According to Colin Brown in *The New International Dictionary of New Testament Theology*, "*tekton* could equally mean 'mason' or 'smith'…or it could mean that Joseph and Jesus were builders, so that both carpentry and masonry would have been among their skills…" (Volume I, p. 279)

[10] Deuteronomy 6:4-9 is at the core of Jewish belief: "Hear, O Israel: The LORD our God, the LORD is one. Love the LORD your God with all your heart and with all your soul and with all your strength. These commandments that I give you today are to be upon your hearts. Impress them on your children. Talk about them when you sit at home and when you walk along the road, when you lie down and when you get up. Tie them as symbols on your hands and bind them on your foreheads. Write them on the doorframes of your houses and on your gates."

[11] Hillel was active from 20 BCE through 10 CE (see Brad Young, *Meet the Rabbis*, p. 40). Thus, if Jesus was born in 4BCE, as generally believed, Hillel could have been teaching Torah in the Temple courts when the twelve-year-old Jesus joined the discussion.

[12] See Philippians 2:5-11.

him after his baptism.[13] Jesus worked miracles with the Father's permission in the power of the Spirit.

In the Matthew 13 passage cited above, as well as in an earlier episode in Nazareth,[14] Jesus' hometown acquaintances were dumbfounded when they perceived Yeshua's spiritual depth. In his early years, Christ must have kept a low profile: no miracles, no Messianic claims, no astounding teaching. After his baptism, the time was right and Yeshua launched his ministry.

> *His Holy Nature*

In modern society, one who lived a sinless lifestyle would be conspicuous. Yeshua's holiness, however, could be discreet in a culture dominated by the pursuit of godliness. His fun-loving nature and skepticism about man-made traditions would have deflected some attention away from his perfected godliness.

Being conceived miraculously, his human nature was genetically connected to ours, yet not tainted by inherited sin. We are all curious about the life of Jesus before he began his ministry, but our curiosity cannot be satisfied. Christians have learned to live with many unanswered questions about how the two natures of Jesus interacted together, for example. Could he have potentially sinned? How could he be tempted? How could a human – even a perfect one – live a sinless lifestyle when the rest of us cannot even live a

---

[13] See Matthew 3:13-17.
[14] See Luke 4:14-30.

sinless day? God, in his wisdom, has revealed everything we *need* to know, not everything we want to know.[15]

Galilean Jews were noted for their spiritual zeal and a compassionate, practical form of Judaism. This region produced hundreds of rabbis who roamed the countryside with their bands of disciples.[16] The culture throughout Israel primed men to surrender weeks, months, or sometimes a year or two to follow a rabbi and thus "enter the kingdom of heaven" as they studied Torah.[17]

The willingness of Jesus' disciples to drop their occupations for a time and follow a sage loses its mysterious edge when we realize that this was a typical scenario. Godly Jewish men had been doing similar things for centuries. Thus rabbis and their disciples were valued by the culture, and the locals considered it a privilege to house and feed them as they journeyed from village to village. The early church followed in this tradition, but they carefully screened teachers they housed to assure that they recognized the deity and humanity of Jesus Christ.[18] We will develop the theme of discipleship and the rabbi-disciple relationship in Chapter 10.

---

[15] Deuteronomy 29:29 (NASB) makes this clear: "The secret things belong to the LORD our God, but the things revealed belong to us and to our sons forever, that we may observe all the words of this law."

[16] David Bivin, in his excellent volume, *New Light on the Difficult Words of Jesus*, writes, "Not only does the number of first-century Galilean rabbis exceed the number of Judean rabbis, but the moral and ethical quality of their teaching is still considered more highly than that of their Judean counterparts…the Galileans could be seen as the religious conservatives of the period…" (pp. 3-4).

[17] *New Light on the Difficult Words of Jesus*, pp. 17-21.

[18] 2 John 1:7-10 (NASB) provides an example of screening in the early church: "For many deceivers have gone out into the world, those who do not acknowledge Jesus Christ as coming in the flesh This is the

> *Questions Raised About the Word of God*

This "hypostatic union" means we believe that Yeshua is both God and man. This raises a question: If Jesus was God, was every word he uttered the "Word of God?" If Christ asked brother James to "pass the biscuits," was that request inspired?

I think we need to make a distinction between (1) words a divine Person has spoken, (2) the inspired words of a divine Person, and (3) Scripture.

Consider the first category, "words a divine Person has spoken." This includes whatever God the Father, Son, or Holy Spirit have said to one another, to angels, or to men.[19] Many of these words – though true and perfect – were intended only for the moment.

The *inspired* words of a divine Person are not merely true, but impregnated with a special power and purpose (Isaiah 55:10-11). But not all inspired words have been preserved.[20] When we discuss God's written Word (Scripture), we mean God's preserved and inspired word.

The Scriptures provide a blueprint for all we need in the realm of spiritual maturity (2

---

deceiver and the antichrist. Watch yourselves, that you do not lose what we have accomplished, but that you may receive a full reward. Anyone who goes too far and does not abide in the teaching of Christ, does not have God; the one who abides in the teaching, he has both the Father and the Son. If anyone comes to you and does not bring this teaching, do not receive him into your house, and do not give him a greeting…"

[19] Though some of these words were both inspired and Scripture, it is interesting to note that the creation of the universe could be attributed to a conversation between the Persons of the Trinity.

[20] I Corinthians 14 makes clear that prophesying was an important function in the infant church. Prophesying is often defined as either inspired speech or inspired thought. Yet these many prophecies (some true, others false) have not been preserved. The First Testament mentions many prophets whose words are not recorded in Scripture. For example, in I Kings 14, Ahab speaks poorly of Ahijah the prophet. This means that Ahijah had previously prophesied, but these words were not recorded. In I Samuel 28:6, Saul inquired of the prophets but received no answer. Thus nameless prophets dot the First Testament.

Timothy 3:16-17). Thus the Scriptures are the full composite of all the inspired teaching God has determined perennial and essential.

Yeshua spoke many inspired words, but only some of them have been preserved as Scripture.[21] From a human perspective, we can assume that the Gospel writers chose to include portions they considered relevant to the Christian community or for evangelism. What do we mean by assuming all Scripture is inspired? Although many conservative Christians claim to believe in *verbal, plenary inspiration*, some who make this claim really believe in a theory called "dictation." This theory maintains that God dictated to the Biblical authors. In other words, they essentially fell into a trance and were passive. Writing Scripture utilized their wrists, but not their minds. In contrast, *verbal plenary inspiration means that God guided the authors and worked with their minds to insure that what they said was in accord with what God wanted said. God saw to it that the words they chose accurately conveyed the thoughts God wanted to convey.*[22] I operate from the premise of verbal, plenary inspiration.

I believe that God typically worked through and with the human minds of the Scriptural authors. Some texts, like the 613 commandments of the Torah, were indeed dictated, but

---

[21] This is suggested by John 21:25, "And there are also many other things which Jesus did, which if they were written in detail, I suppose that even the world itself would not contain the books that would be written." One "thing" Jesus did much of is teaching.

[22] See Grudem, Wayne, *Systematic Theology*, pp. 80-81.

dictation is not the rule. Thus we believe the entire Bible to be the Word of God, but much of it is simultaneously the Word of God AND the word of godly men.[23]

Plenary inspiration means that all Scripture is *equally* inspired. David's Psalms, the words Paul penned, and the words Jesus spoke are equally inspired. This is a departure from Jewish belief, in which the entire *Tanakh* (Old Testament) is considered inspired, but the Torah is considered more inspired than the writings or prophets.[24]

If we assume that God used the human mind of Paul in the process of inspiration, why should we think it improbable that God used the human mind of Jesus in similar fashion? If so, are there clues that help us penetrate that mind? I answer with a resounding "yes!"

On the Other Hand, Jesus Was Similar to Other Rabbis

Although we refer to Yeshua as a "rabbi," we do so in neither the modern nor most ancient use of the word. The term has changed meaning since he ministered on earth and the term kept changing.[25] *The Second Testament* usually refers to "scribes" or "teachers of the Law." Over the centuries, the term "rabbi" became the common nomenclature for such scholars. Schurer comments about two major rabbis whose lives overlapped with Jesus:

---

[23] See Daniel Wallace's paper, "Is Intra-Canonical Theological Development Compatible with a High Bibliology?" for further study on this subject.

[24] "To the Pentateuch or Torah a higher degree of divine inspiration is accordingly ascribed than to the Prophets and Hagiographa" from the *Jewish Encyclopedia* article on "Inspiration," http://www.jewishencyclopedia.com, accessed 11-11-09.

[25] The modern rabbi is part of the professional, salaried clergy caste, usually associated with the ministry of a specific synagogue. This was not the situation in the days of Yeshua or in the centuries immediately afterward.

> Hillel and Shammai were never called Rabbis, nor is [rabbi] found in the New Testament except as an actual address. The word does not seem to have been used as a title till after the time of Christ.[26]

The term "sage" is often used for the older rabbis, the great teachers a century or two before Yeshua's time and those several centuries afterward. Since the term "sage" was later replaced by "rabbi," we have chosen to adjust our terminology accordingly. Brad Young defines "sage:"

> A wise teacher who was knowledgeable in all areas of Jewish law and literature. Sages preached and taught the Torah during the Talmudic and Mishnaic periods. The term may refer to both rabbis from the land of Israel as well as Babylonian ravs.[27]

➤ *Blinded by Our Assumptions*

My wife is an artist, and I myself enjoy viewing artwork. While touring Italy, we had the privilege of savoring some of the world's great masterpieces. Since most of these famous artworks involved a religious theme, it was also amusing to notice how Italian artists (whose knowledge was restricted by what was familiar to them) portrayed Biblical stories. For example, we know that Jewish ritual immersion (baptism) involved complete submersion in water. Yet the artists – knowing only Roman Catholic practice and virtually nothing about Jewish backgrounds – picture John the Baptist pouring a few drops of water on Yeshua's head. Mary was Jewish through and through. Yet she is

---

[26] Emil Schurer, *A History of the Jewish People in the Time of Christ*, p. 315.
[27] Brad Young, *Meet the Rabbis*, p. 232.

frequently portrayed as blond-haired and blue-eyed; those are not typical Jewish features.[28]

The inaccuracies we see in religious artwork serve as a visual object lesson: when we make assumptions about our faith – including Yeshua's teachings – based upon the traditions surrounding us, we can easily miss the mark; pinpointed accuracy requires knowledge of first century Judaism. After all, the culture and beliefs of first century Israel is the backdrop for Jesus' life and teachings. Some of us may tend to inflate the value of ideas formulated centuries after Yeshua walked the earth while deflating the importance of the actual context of the *Second Testament*.

The idea that many of Christ's teachings were not unusual – but mainstream Jewish teaching – is an old, yet relatively new idea. It is old because first century Jewish believers recognized this,[29] yet it is new because second century gentile church leaders discarded this key, a key which has only recently been retrieved.[30] In this book, I hope to use "The Midrash Key" to expand the context and unlock some of the nuances of Yeshua's teaching.

---

[28] Alexander Hislop attributes this to the paganization of Christianity as it embraced and included deities from other religions: "In a land of dark-eyed beauties, with raven locks, the Madonna was always represented with blue eyes and golden hair, a complexion entirely different from the Jewish complexion, which naturally would have been supposed to belong to the mother of our Lord, but which precisely agrees with that which all antiquity attributes to the goddess queen of Babylon…" *The Two Babylons*, p. 85. Although Hislop's work is speculative and he sometimes presents theories as fact, he does argue the case that pagan elements found their way into the Christian Church –even if some of his arguments are questionable.

[29] For an example, see David H. Stern's *Restoring the Jewishness of the Gospel*, pp. 43-60.

[30] Mark Kinzer, in *Post-Missionary Messianic Judaism*, documents this thoroughly on pp.183-201.

> *A Typical Scenario*

Like the Italian artists, the general "picture" assumed by most of Christendom for about 1900 years has missed the mark. It may sound something like this:

Jesus came to his own people, and preached out against Judaism. He taught that the whole system was corrupt, the Mosaic Law was a bad thing, and he came to found an entirely new religion based upon loving God and loving one's neighbor, a new concept he delivered to the hypocritical Jewish people.

Because the Jews were so wicked, Jesus left Judaism[31] and founded Christianity. In resentment of him, the Jews rose up and crucified him. Then they persecuted the church. God was so angry with the Jews, that he cancelled all the promises of land and glory he had made to that nation, and replaced the Jewish people with the church. Jews are, by nature, evil people and deserve the suffering they have experienced for their evil treatment of Jesus.

> *An Alternate Scenario*

The above scenario is what many Christians have believed and were taught. Reading the Bible apart from its historical and Jewish context can birth such a belief system. We could point out specific verses that seem to bolster some of these misunderstandings. In

---

[31] John 7:1, poorly translated in the King James Version, may reflect the anti-Semitism of the translators or may have merely been a poor translation that nonetheless propagated the belief that Jesus had forsaken Judaism. It reads, "After these things Jesus walked in Galilee: for he would not walk in **Jewry**, because the Jews sought to kill him."

addition, the prejudices and anti-Semitism espoused by important church leaders throughout the centuries have embedded these misunderstandings deep into the theology and viewpoint of much of Christendom. Here is my alternative scenario. I have noted the distinctions between mine and the previous scenario through use of italics:

Yeshua came to his own people, and preached out against *the hypocrites within* Judaism, *as did many other Jewish rabbis and leaders; most of the Jewish people agreed that the problem was real. This is why Jesus was able to get away with turning over the tables in the temple courtyards on two occasions: many people experienced similar frustration with their corrupt leaders who were in collaboration with their Roman oppressors.*

He taught that the entire system was *not* corrupt, **encouraging** *his followers to obey the rulings of the rabbis who "sat in the seat of Moses."*[32] He taught that the Law was *good*; *he had not come to abolish it, but to fulfill (properly interpret and apply)it;*[33] he came *to restore Judaism to its foundation,* based upon loving God and loving one's neighbor, *an old* concept *from Deuteronomy embraced by many rabbis at that time. He had a special love for the Jewish people, and he wept over the judgment that awaited them because of their unbelief, yet he prophesied about a future time when the Jewish people would welcome him as Messiah.*

---

[32] See Matthew 23:1-3
[33] See Matthew 5:17

Because the corrupt and powerful Jewish leaders rejected him, and because most Jews were uncertain about him, Jesus accumulated those Jews who did believe in him, and began his Messianic- Jewish church (assembly) with this remnant. Later, in the book of Acts, he revealed that this assembly would include gentile believers as well.

In resentment *(and fear that the Romans would view Jesus as a political threat and bring more oppression to Judea)*[34] of him, *the corrupt Jewish minority who held the power secretly called an illegal trial. They selectively invited leaders they assumed would embrace their dubious scheme. They collaborated with the Romans and – while the Jewish people were distracted celebrating Passover–* crucified him.

The Jewish people, as a whole, would not have approved of his trial or crucifixion. Whereas they were not necessarily convinced that Jesus was the Messiah, they did view him as a notable rabbi and a good man. While many were undecided, the Palm Sunday crowd who had come from the north (Galilee) and Bethany remained faithful to the Lord. Later, in the Book of Acts, many priests (Acts 6:7) and Pharisees (Acts 15:5) came to believe in Yeshua.

---

[34] The ESV of John 11:47-52 is an important section that reveals one main motivation on the part of Jewish leaders to kill Yeshua: "So the chief priests and the Pharisees gathered the Council and said, 'What are we to do? For this man performs many signs. If we let him go on like this, everyone will believe in him, and the Romans will come and take away both our place and our nation.' But one of them, Caiaphas, who was high priest that year, said to them, 'You know nothing at all. Nor do you understand that it is better for you that one man should die for the people, not that the whole nation should perish.' He did not say this of his own accord, but being high priest that year he prophesied that Jesus would die for the nation, and not for the nation only, but also to gather into one the children of God who are scattered abroad."

Some of the same powerful leaders who hated Jesus persecuted the church, *while the godly leaders, like Rabbi Gamaliel, opposed persecution (Acts 5:33-39).* God's anger burned against Jewish unbelief. Allowing one generation's time for repentance (40 years), Yahweh *brought about the destruction of Jerusalem and grafted many gentile believers into the church to make Israel jealous.*[35] *God will one day fulfill* the promises he had made to that nation, *because he is faithful, sovereign,*[36] *and not dependent upon human fickleness. He has not* replaced the Jews with the church. *Believing Jews as well as believing gentiles are part of the Body of the Messiah, the church. When it comes to salvation, God covenants on an individual basis (John 1:11-12). Unbelieving Jews are lost and in need of salvation, just as unbelieving gentiles are lost and in need of salvation. But God has a special destiny for the generation of Jewish people living in the "end times."*[37] *The church is connected to and draws her sustenance from Israel, yet God's promises to the genetic descendents of Jacob stand.* Jews are, at times, *a stubborn*

---

[35] Romans 11:13-15 (New KJV): "For I speak to you Gentiles; inasmuch as I am an apostle to the Gentiles, I magnify my ministry, if by any means I may provoke to jealousy *those who are* my flesh and save some of them. For if their being cast away *is* the reconciling of the world, what *will* their acceptance *be* but life from the dead?"

[36] Jeremiah 31:35-37 (KJV) could not be worded more dogmatically: "Thus saith the LORD, which giveth the sun for a light by day, and the ordinances of the moon and of the stars for a light by night, which divideth the sea when the waves thereof roar; The LORD of hosts is his name: If those ordinances depart from before me, saith the LORD, then the seed of Israel also shall cease from being a nation before me for ever. Thus saith the LORD; If heaven above can be measured, and the foundations of the earth searched out beneath, I will also cast off all the seed of Israel for all that they have done, saith the LORD."

[37] Romans 11:26, Zechariah 12.

and *stiff-necked people*[38] and *make wonderful examples of God's grace to the undeserving.*

> ➤ *Others Have Already Documented A Similar Paradigm*

Messianic Jewish and Jewish Roots authorities have produced a wealth of volumes and articles to argue the case above. Especially noteworthy are *Restoring the Jewishness of the Gospel* by David Stern, *Jesus, the Jewish Theologian* by Brad Young, *Yeshua: A Guide to the Real Jesus and the Original Church* by Ron Moseley, and *They Loved the Torah* by David Friedman. In this volume, I hope to build upon these assumptions and put them to practical work. I will elaborate upon some of the above in later chapters and footnote in greater detail.

I believe when Yeshua preached to the Jewish crowds, he did so out of love and respect. To the Samaritan woman at the well, Jesus was transparent about his view of the Jewish people and Judaism, "You Samaritans worship what you do not know; we worship what we do know, for salvation is from the Jews."[39] Note that Jesus used the term "we," thus including himself as a Jew.

He cherished the Law and sought to apply it to his listeners, and he fully engaged in the debates of his day. Yeshua was unlike any other rabbi, yet he was more like his rabbinic peers than most Christians imagine. He validated the rulings of other rabbis; he sided

---

[38] See Deuteronomy 9:6-13 where God so labels the Jewish people of the time.
[39] John 4:22

with one particular school of rabbis most times, but not always. He talked about what fellow rabbis talked about, the "hot issues" of the day. Sometimes he found himself caught in the crossfire between competing schools of thought (the conflict between the School of Hillel – *Bet Hillel*, and the School of Shammai – *Bet Shammai*). Most of his teachings were consistent with mainstream Judaism.

Many others have demonstrated that Jesus taught in typical rabbinic fashion, using a method known as *Midrash*. But I want to go beyond merely asserting that Jesus used *Midrash*; I want to take *Midrash* from the mothballs of scholarly closets and use it to expand the context of Yeshua's teaching. As a result, we can understand him better and follow him more closely.

Since many of Yeshua's sermons were *Midrashim*, we can dispel the misguided idea that Jesus preached "topical" sermons. We will observe that he actually preached expository sermons with an emphasis upon applying the principle of the text. He started with an Old Testament text, looked for a principle within the text (sometimes the main principle, sometimes a secondary principle), and then applied the *principle* to his day. If this is so – and if some of his teachings are based on Hebraic expressions that lose their edge when translated into Greek or English[40] – then someone has to do the "grunt work" of locating the starting point, the *First Testament* text Yeshua used for *Midrash*. Then one must

---

[40] See *Understanding the Difficult Words of Jesus* by David Bivin and Roy Blizzard, Jr.; Analyzing the Hebraic expressions that do not quite translate into Greek and English make up the bulk of Bivin and Blizzard's book.

examine how Christ applied principles from that text *as Second Testament* teaching. Needless to say, this is not an exact science; some guesswork is involved. But we are not without clues, as we shall demonstrate.

What Is A *Midrash*?

> *A Midrash is a Jewish Way to Interpret a Text and Apply It as a Sermon*

It is time to hone our understanding of *Midrash,* and our use of the term. The word *Midrash* is pronounced "mid-rosh," and can mean a variety of things (as explained in The Introduction). In this book, the term *Midrash* simply applies to the process of a New Testament author or speaker interpreting and applying an Old Testament text.

Walter Kaiser discusses the beginnings of *Midrash:*

> The Midrashic method of exegesis had its genesis in public lectures and homilies. The lecturer would set forth the theme of his homily by reading from a passage of Scripture which enunciated the truth on which he wished to speak. He would then illustrate that truth with a parable and enforce it with a saying that was already popular with the people.[41]

P*reaching* in the "Midrash style" (which emphasized applying the broad principle behind a Scripture to a variety of current situations) did not change much between the first and later centuries, but how texts were *interpreted* did change.

The Jewish Encyclopedia offers us the typical definition of *Midrash* as it is commonly used today:

---

[41] Walter C. Kaiser, *Toward An Exegetical Theology*, p. 53.

> In contradistinction to literal interpretation, subsequently called "*Pesha*" ... the term "*Midrash*" designates an exegesis which, going more deeply than the mere literal sense, attempts to penetrate into the spirit of the Scriptures, to examine the text from all sides, and thereby to derive interpretations which are not immediately obvious. The *Talmud* (Sanh. 34b) compares this kind of Midrashic exposition to a hammer which awakens the slumbering sparks in the rock.[42]

Another Jewish source defines *Midrash* as, "The discovery of meaning other than literal in the Bible."[43]

The term *Midrash* designated less literal interpretation over time, but in the early first century, *Midrash* included both literal and less literal interpretations and was not necessarily distinguished from *Pesha (Peshat)*. Longenecker comments:

> Evidently, the early rabbis felt that their exegesis – whatever their methods later might be called, and however we might classify them – was a setting forth of the essential meaning of the biblical texts and therefore to be identified as either *Peshat* or *Midrash,* with the two terms considered to be roughly equivalent.[44]

Thus, during Christ's ministry, the distinction between *Midrash* and *Peshat* was not as pronounced as it later became. For our purposes, we should think of an early first century *Midrash* as a Jewish sermon that resembles, in some ways, a modern expository sermon. The main point in such a sermon may or may not focus upon the particulars in the text, but the principle behind the particulars is in the spotlight.[45] In other instances, *a little-noticed implication* might become the emphasis, as is the case in Matthew 22:31-32

---

[42] *The Jewish Encyclopedia*, article (by Jacobs and Horowitz) on "Midrash," www.jewishencyclopedia.com, accessed 11-11-09.
[43] R. J. Zwi Werblowsky and Geoffrey Wigoder, editors, *The Encyclopedia of Jewish Religion*, p. 261.
[44] Richard N. Longenecker, in *Biblical Exegesis in the Apostolic Period*, p. 18.
[45] Yeshua and the New Testament authors seem to follow *Hillel's Seven Rules*, his principles for Biblical interpretation. They are discussed by Walter Kaiser, *op. cit.*, pp. 53-55.

(KJV). In this text, Yeshua uses *Midrash* to refute the Sadducees by calling attention to an unnoticed implication from a text. Although not the main thought in the *First Testament* text quoted, Jesus' *Midrash* follows logically:

> But as touching the resurrection of the dead, have ye not read that which was spoken unto you by God, saying, I am the God of Abraham, and the God of Isaac, and the God of Jacob? God is not the God of the dead, but of the living.

> ➢ *The Midrash Technique Included Constructing Fences*

In order to apply the principle of the text to contemporary issues, a sage would sometimes expand the boundaries of a text. In an attempt to add a safety margin, the rabbi would "build a fence"[46] around one of the 613 commands of the Torah. Yeshua clearly built fences in the *Sermon on the Mount*; he built a fence around marital faithfulness by encouraging his followers to nip adultery in the heart. He did the same with murder: if we refuse to hate another in our hearts, we are unlikely to commit actual murder.

> ➢ *Midrash Included Liberal Use of Parables*

Closely associated with the *Midrash* technique is the frequent use of parables. David Bivin writes about Jesus' teaching ministry and style. The quotation addresses two themes: the use of parables and discipleship. We will split Bivin's words between two sub-headings:

---

[46] "Be deliberate in judgment, raise up many disciples, and make a fence around the Torah..." *Mishnah, Ethics of the Fathers*, 1:1.

> Parables such as Jesus used were extremely prevalent among ancient Jewish sages, and over 4,000 of them have survived in rabbinic literature…[47]

> ➢ *Midrash Was Used in the Context of Disciple-Making*

> … the rabbis of Jesus' day spent much of their time traveling throughout the country to communicate their teachings and interpretations of Scripture. An itinerant rabbi was the norm rather than the exception. Hundreds and perhaps thousands of such rabbis circulated in the land of Israel in the first century.
> To "make many disciples" was one of the three earliest sayings recorded in the *Mishnah*, and perhaps the highest calling of a rabbi. Often he would select and train large numbers of disciples, but he was perfectly willing to teach as few as two or three students. It is recorded that the Apostle Paul's teacher Gamaliel had one thousand disciples who studied with him.[48]

Following a rabbi meant taking leave from one's career for weeks or months to follow the sage as he traveled the countryside. The disciple would listen as the rabbi taught the crowds who eagerly gathered to receive spiritual nurture. The faithful disciple might one day himself become a sage with his own band of disciples.

The disciple would memorize the teachings of his rabbi. All devout Jews would have already memorized the Torah in their youth, so this knowledge was assumed. The disciple would listen to the casual discussions between his rabbi and fellow disciples; he might ask questions, help the sage by teaching smaller groups, and even emulate his mannerisms and habits. Rabbis would repeat their same teachings to new crowds; this would help the disciple memorize his rabbi's words.

---

[47] Bivin, David, *New Light on the Difficult Words* of Jesus, pp 12-14.
[48] *Ibid.*

> *Midrashim Were to Be Memorized, Negating the Need for a "Q" Document*

When we first read the Synoptic Gospels (Matthew, Mark, and Luke), it was probably not long before we noticed their similarities. It seems obvious that someone "copied" from somebody else. Theologians have postulated a "Q" document –- a missing source of Gospel information from which Matthew, Mark, and Luke drew. [49]

Since there is no proof that the "Q" document exists or ever existed, how can we disprove its existence? I believe we can propose a better explanation for the synoptic similarities, one consistent with reality and not imagined.

If we understand the Jewish concept of discipleship, we can better explain the similarities between Matthew, Mark, and Luke. In first century Judaism, a disciple's primary job was to memorize his sage's words, most of which were *Midrashim*. Day and night, disciples would rehearse what the master said, practicing to attain perfection.

If we embrace that a disciple's main task was to memorize the teachings of his sage, then Jesus' disciples would have passed on memorized tractates, complete with descriptions and event details. Since Yeshua repeated similar sermons to differing crowds, the Gospel "quotations" are really summaries, either edited quotations or loose quotations. We should remember that the use of quotation marks is a relatively modern concept. In the Gospels, the difference between summary and exact quotation is unclear. Thus some differences can be explained by how much was summarized.

---

[49] *Ibid.*, pp.5-7, 33-38

If you became a Hebrew Christian in 50 AD, you would be expected to invest much time and energy toward memorizing Jesus' words and works. These words would have been handed down to you from those who were disciples before you (cf. Hebrews 2:3-4). Being a disciple meant being a learner and *memorizer*. We will examine the subject of discipleship more closely in chapter 10.

These memorized accounts make up a large percentage of the synoptics – particularly the wordings and events that converge in Matthew, Mark, and Luke. Incidentally, none of this precludes the work of the Holy Spirit. Understanding some of the mechanics of preservation does not eliminate the divine mystery or providence of inspiration. From a practical perspective, we might envy the early believers for their diligence as they hid vast portions of God's Word in their hearts.

The Secret to Enhanced Understanding of Yeshua's Teachings

The key to good interpretation begins with first locating the passage that Jesus is expositing. This will be the process for the rest of this book.

We must take into account that our Lord spoke for hours at a time, but we have only a few minutes worth of materials recorded in the various Gospel texts. Thus, locating the *First Testament* text under scrutiny is like a shot of hermeneutical adrenaline to give us MORE CONTEXT. We can examine Yeshua's words and note the clues that lead us back to the Torah; once we find the Torah (or *First Testament*) passage, we can see how Yeshua distilled and applied the Torah portion under study.

In addition, we can increase the context even more by examining the rabbinic debate of the era via the *Mishnah*, *Talmud*, and other ancient sources purported to go back in time to the era of Yeshua's ministry.

Yeshua's Teaching: Midrashim Galore

A casual Bible reader might note the seeming contradictions between the moral instruction Jesus offers his followers on the *Sermon on the Mount* and the writings of Paul – or even the Old Testament, for example. The reason for these apparent discrepancies is not because Yeshua disagreed with Moses, or that Paul was taking liberties Jesus never intended. Nor is the *Sermon on the Mount* reserved for end-time believers during the Tribulation period. The fact that scholars propose such extreme means to address the *Sermon on the Mount* evidences the chasm between those texts and the writings of Paul or John, for example.

Whereas it is true that some of the context of the *Sermon on the Mount* (*SOM*) applies specifically to first century Jews (such as "leaving your gift on the altar"), the fact that the Synoptic Gospels include portions from the *SOM* implies its relevance to the Christian community. These apparent discrepancies disappear once we increase the context.

Conclusion

If we interpret Jesus' words in light of the originating *First Testament* text, and if we understand the rabbinic debates of the era, we can find a *satisfying* and natural way to interpret Yeshua's teachings, including *The Sermon on the Mount*, for example. We will find that the teachings of Christ neither contradict the *Tanakh* nor other portions of the *Second Testament*. Let's begin our explorations.

Chapter 2: The Problem Within (Deuteronomy 5:28-29, 10:12-16; 30:6 with Mark 7:6-23)

Deuteronomy: Yeshua's Favorite Book

Pastors in particular are likely to name one of the Pastoral Epistles – like I Timothy – as their favorite book of the Bible. Believers who have been sorely tested with painful trials gravitate toward the Psalms. The Gospels document Yeshua quoting Deuteronomy more than any other portion of Scripture, so we might postulate that this was his favorite book. I believe the evidence suggests that Jesus developed more of his *Midrashim* from Deuteronomy than any other book.

The ethical system we call the *Sermon on the Mount* finds much of its origin in Deuteronomy. Thus Christians who seek to live by Jesus' principles are living by Deuteronomy – whether aware of it or not.

Deuteronomy, the final book of the Torah, fades in after Israel's forty-year wilderness sentence has been served. The previous generation tested God's patience, embraced cynical and critical attitudes, and insulted Yahweh's integrity. As we enter more deeply into the book, we realize that Moses – the ancient, seasoned leader – is preparing to meet his Maker.

A new generation has assumed the reins, a generation that reverenced and welcomed God. Faithful Joshua and Caleb would lead the Hebrews to commence the conquest of Canaan. Despite capable leaders and willing attitudes, the children of Israel needed to be strengthened spiritually. Yahweh directed Moses to provide the people with a fresh, nuanced version of God's Law: the Book of Deuteronomy.

> ➤ *The Limitations of This Study*

We cannot discover *all* the teachings Yeshua may have squeezed from the Book of Deuteronomy, but I will highlight some *Midrashim* likely sourced in Deuteronomy. In some chapters, we will begin with other "mother texts" outside of Deuteronomy, so we are not limiting ourselves to only *Midrashim* derived from Deuteronomy.

I hope the many "coincidences" between Deuteronomy and Gospel texts will persuade skeptical readers that these similarities are not merely coincidental. Even the most suspicious must agree that Jesus developed *themes* found in Deuteronomy. So even if we occasionally err by labeling a teaching as *Midrash* when it is merely a common theme, what harm have we done? We are still drawing our beliefs from an intelligent, faithful interpretation of God's Word. We have little to lose, but much to gain.

Our Biggest Problem: Man's Sinful Heart

> ➤ *Man Has a Heart Problem*

Our first proposed Midrash is a foundational theme in Jesus' teaching ministry, "The Problem Within." Yeshua's teaching about evil emerging from within the human heart in

Mark 7:20-23 finds it origin in a splattering of passages from Deuteronomy, particularly 5:28-29, 10:12-16 and 30:6, in my opinion. We will quote the texts below.

The central idea in both Deuteronomy and Mark passages is a shared one. The human heart – the internal, invisible center of our being – is in a bad way. It desperately needs a supernatural work of redemption and regeneration. We should not diagnose man's central problem as his external behavior but his internal nature; his outward actions flow from the heart within. Addressing this problem is two-fold: we need spiritual life (regeneration), but once regenerate, we need to constantly yield to God.

Note the content of Deuteronomy 5:28-29; 10:12-16, 30:6, quoted below; I have used bold face for emphasis.

> 5:28 – 29, The LORD heard you when you spoke to me and the LORD said to me, "I have heard what this people said to you. Everything they said was good. **Oh, that their hearts would be inclined to fear me** and keep all my commands always, so that it might go well with them and their children forever!
>
> 10:12-16, And now, O Israel, what does the LORD your God ask of you but to fear the LORD your God, to walk in all his ways, to love him, to serve the LORD your God with all your heart and with all your soul, and to observe the LORD's commands and decrees that I am giving you today for your own good?
>
> To the LORD your God belong the heavens, even the highest heavens, the earth and everything in it. Yet the LORD set his affection on your forefathers and loved them, and he chose you, their descendants, above all the nations, as it is today. **Circumcise your hearts, therefore,** and do not be stiff-necked any longer.
>
> 30:6, **The LORD your God will circumcise your hearts** and the hearts of your descendants, so that you may love him with all your heart and with all your soul, and live.

Take notice that God longed for his people to willingly serve him with undivided hearts. Bible history records the sad facts: the Hebrews experienced occasional bursts of faith and zeal, but these were negated by long-term unfaithfulness. In many eras of Israelite history, the masses turned away from Yahweh after other gods. In other instances, they outwardly worshiped Yahweh, but their hearts were far from him. This corporate inclination toward a divided heart does not surface out of nowhere. It began on an individual, personal basis.

> *Regeneration: Man's Responsibility or God's Sovereignty?*

These Deuteronomy passages underscore the paradox between man's responsibility and God's sovereignty, a paradox prominent in the New Testament. We can note two *seemingly* contradictory assertions: *God* is the one who must perform spiritual heart surgery because the human heart needs a supernatural touch (30:6); yet, in 10:12-16, personal responsibility to circumcise one's *own* heart stares us in the face. So which is it? The answer is "both of the above."

In theory, we can make the choice to awaken ourselves from spiritual hibernation and arise to spiritual life. The sovereign hand of God stealthily moves beyond our choices. We can honestly demand that the lost be born-again,[50] but we are also free to announce John 6:44, "No one can come to me [Yeshua] unless the Father who sent me draws him; and I will raise him up on the last day..." (NASB).

---

[50] See John 3:7

The rejection of Messiah by the Jewish people was likewise both a matter of individual responsibility and God's sovereign plan. Few challenge that the Jewish people chose to reject Yeshua as Messiah: "He came to that which was his own, but his own did not receive him..."[51] Yet many experience discomfort to read, "He has blinded their eyes and deadened their hearts, so they can neither see with their eyes, nor understand with their hearts, nor turn—and I would heal them."[52].

After "circumcision of the heart," God's Word no longer seems a burden to bear but a delight to enjoy. This enthusiasm does not apply, however, to the man made additions religious zealots have attached to the Torah, nor does it apply to misuse of the Law.[53] Forcing Torah portions intended for Israel upon gentile believers, for example, is one such misuse.[54]

Psalm 119, the longest chapter in the Bible, depicts how the regenerate believer loves and views the Word; absorbing oneself in the Word has moved from tedium to pleasure, from chore to recreation. The difference is the *disposition of the heart.*

In Mark 7, perhaps Yeshua interjected another related *Midrash* based upon the prophet Jeremiah. Jeremiah's piercing words still ring true: "The heart is deceitful above all things, and desperately wicked: who can know it?" (Jeremiah 17:9, KJV). We tend to

---

[51] John 1:11
[52] John 12:40
[53] We will elaborate and document this theme later.
[54] See Acts 15:28

forget instances when we wrong others, but we remember when others wrong us. We think we are objective, but we convince ourselves that our transgressions are understandable responses to how others (or life) have treated us.

Regeneration is the beginning of becoming a new creation, but not the end. Both testaments discuss the challenge of a divided heart. In Psalm 86:11, David petitioned Yahweh, "Teach me your way, O LORD, and I will walk in your truth; give me an *undivided heart*, that I may fear your name." Even King David experienced the struggle within. Though regenerate, he understood the fickleness within.

First Testament Scriptures describe regeneration as "circumcision of the heart," whereas the *Second Testament* uses the terminology of New Birth.[55] Regeneration exerts a great transforming influence upon believers, but Yeshua's disciples still struggle.

> *Battling Kidneys: Man Has Two Competing Inclinations*

The *Talmud* is a vast written collection of ancient rabbinic teaching. We may also refer to it as the "Oral Law." Rabbis and their disciples orally transmitted the oldest part of the *Talmud*, the *Mishnah*, for centuries. This transmission began around 200 BC. *The Babylonian Talmud* (the most quoted version of the *Talmud*) continues to reflect mainstream Jewish thought through the early Christian centuries. It is a massive work with perhaps 3.5 million words, divided into "tractates." The *Talmud* certainly does not

---

[55] For a recommended treatment on this subject, see James M. Hamilton, "Were Old Covenant Believers Indwelt by the Holy Spirit?" *Themelios 30* (2004), 12-22. Available at the Southern Baptist Theological Seminary website, http://jimhamilton.files.wordpress.com/2008/06/them30-1.pdf, accessed 7-3-10.

reflect the views of all Jewish perspectives from Jesus' time, but it does reflect mainstream Rabbinic Judaism. According to the *Talmud,*

> Our Rabbis taught: Man has two kidneys, one of which prompts him to good, the other to evil; and it is natural to suppose that the good one is on his right side and the bad one on his left, as it is written, A wise man's understanding is at his right hand, but a fool's understanding is at his left…[56]

The First Testament word we translate as "heart" is usually the word for kidneys. Both the heart and kidneys are physical pictures used to represent our "inner" spiritual (and invisible) being, our very souls. Since we have two natures – two inclinations – our sometimes inconsistent walk with the Lord reflects our internal conflict.

> ➢ *Yeshua Develops the "Heart Problem" Theme*

In Mark 7:6-23 (ESV), we see that Yeshua does not only build upon the "heart theme," but the context suggests that he does so from Deuteronomy. The text reads:

> And he said to them, "Well did Isaiah prophesy of you hypocrites, as it is written, "'This people honors me with their lips, but their heart is far from me; in vain do they worship me, teaching as doctrines the commandments of men.'
>
> You leave the commandment of God and hold to the tradition of men."
>
> And he said to them, "You have a fine way of rejecting the commandment of God in order to establish your tradition! For Moses said, 'Honor your father and your mother'; and, 'Whoever reviles father or mother must surely die.' But you say, 'If a man tells his father or his mother, "Whatever you would have gained from me is Corban"' (that is, given to God)— then you no longer permit him to do anything for his father or mother, thus making void the word of God by your tradition that you have handed down. And many such things you do."

---

[56]*Berakoth, 61a*

> And he called the people to him again and said to them, "Hear me, all of you, and understand: There is nothing outside a person that by going into him can defile him, but the things that come out of a person are what defile him." And when he had entered the house and left the people, his disciples asked him about the parable. And he said to them, "Then are you also without understanding? Do you not see that whatever goes into a person from outside cannot defile him, since it enters not his heart but his stomach, and is expelled?" (Thus he declared all foods clean.) And he said, "What comes out of a person is what defiles him. For from within, out of the heart of man, come evil thoughts, sexual immorality, theft, murder, adultery, coveting, wickedness, deceit, sensuality, envy, slander, pride, foolishness. All these evil things come from within, and they defile a person."

In the context of Mark 7, we discover that Yeshua and his disciples had probably been condemned by the most influential school of Pharisees (*Bet Shammai*). Although Yeshua demonstrated no obligation to side with either *Bet Shammai* or *Bet Hillel*, Jesus frequently agreed with *Bet Hillel*. Here, Yeshua is putting Shammai's disciples in their place; Jesus is arguing with them and advancing the perspective typical of *Bet Hillel*. One constant matter of debate between these schools (and the rabbis in general) involved ranking commands in priority order. That commands were sorted out and prioritized in this manner is seen in action as we peruse Matthew 23:23 (NASB):

> "Woe to you, scribes and Pharisees, hypocrites! For you tithe mint and dill and cumin, and have neglected the weightier provisions of the law: justice and mercy and faithfulness; but these are the things you should have done without neglecting the others."

Sages were to define instances in which lesser commands could be compromised in order to obey more important commands. As already mentioned, the rabbis sought to "build fences" around the commands.[57] One familiar example involves using God's name disrespectfully. Since the Jews feared misusing God's Name (Yahweh), they substituted "Adonai" whenever they would read the name aloud. Modern Jews will often write "G-d" instead of "God" as an additional fence around the fence around this command. Christ argues that canonizing tradition is dangerous because it frequently results in DISPLACING the original intent of Scripture through too many layers of fencing. The focus becomes the "fences" rather than the commandments, and commandments become burdens instead of opportunities. Yeshua argues that violating a rabbi's "fence" is not equivalent to violating God's Word.

What Matters Most: Kosher Food in Contrast to the Heart

> *Yeshua's Midrash Follows the Topical Sequence of Deuteronomy*

In the broader context of Deuteronomy, couched between the repeated emphases upon "the heart," are the kosher (ceremonially clean) laws of Deuteronomy 12. How important are the kosher commands – really? How are they ranked in comparison to issues of the heart? Why did God restrict Israel from pork, rabbit, lobster, shrimp, crab, and squid? Are these really moral issues?

---

[57] See Ann Spangler and Lois Tverberg, *Sitting At the Feet of Rabbi Jesus*, pp. 167-170 for a discussion about "building fences around the Torah."

In Mark 7, Christ affirms that man's main problem is his heart – not what he eats. Thus Yeshua clearly designates priorities. Mark adds a parenthetical *Midrash* of his own based upon the Messiah's words: "thus declaring all food clean."

Jesus communicates that a heart predisposed toward God is more important than a strict kosher diet. For sure, this is not a choice most Jews frequently had to make; for the average Jew, love for God can be demonstrated by obedience, and there was usually no reason why obedience to the greater commands could not include the kosher laws.[58] By ranking the kosher laws below one's heart attitude toward God, Yeshua is not saying that they are mutually exclusive. The issue is which matters *most*.

➢ *Kosher Confusion*

The Scriptural evidence affirms that Jesus, Paul, and the Jewish believers of Acts 21:20-26 continued to eat kosher.[59] Had Jesus ceased observing the kosher laws, his credibility within the Jewish communities – and even with his own disciples – would have been ruined. Like Paul, he met the requirements of blamelessly following the kosher laws. As the sinless Lamb of God, Yeshua fully obeyed the proper interpretation of the Torah. Since both Jesus and Paul were frequently invited to speak in the synagogues, they must have kept themselves kosher. Rejecting the kosher lifestyle would have been interpreted

---

[58] Neglect of this ranking of priorities may have been part of the issue in Galatians 2:11-19. This teaching – that some commands are more important than kosher law – was probably a significant matter once the church began embracing gentiles into the congregations.

[59] This is an important portion of Scripture to study; the author high recommends you contemplate the implications of these verses, interpreting them naturally.

as rampant apostasy; such a guest would never be invited to address a synagogue assembly.

Years later, Peter experienced a monumental vision: a sheet descended from heaven (cf. Acts 10:9ff). Ponder this: even at that time – *years* after Pentecost – *the idea of eating non-kosher food was foreign to Peter's way of thinking*. The lesson of the vision had nothing to do with eating habits (although he was told to "kill and eat" in the vision), but the lesson was about accepting gentile (unclean) *people*: "…God has shown me that I should not call any *man* impure or unclean."[60]

Returning to Mark 7, what does Mark mean: "Jesus declared all foods 'clean'?" David Stern suggests that kosher food was clean *even apart from the ceremonial washings* Jesus' opponents demanded.[61] But a more satisfying interpretation is that Jesus declared food *intrinsically* clean. Food is not in itself a spiritual matter.

In Genesis 9, God gives mankind freedom to eat all kinds of animals – assuming they first drained the blood. Yet for his people Israel, Yahweh *later* created distinct standards to distinguish Jacob's descendents from all the other nations of the earth. The kosher laws contributed toward that end. Kosher restrictions may have some other logical foundation, but the basis is clearly neither moral nor spiritual. Yet, when God has spoken, his demands become spiritual – at least to those for whom God intended those demands. We

---

[60] Acts 10:28b
[61] David H. Stern, *The Jewish New Testament Commentary*, pp. 93.

can say there is something *Jewish* about kosher food – and something *gentile* about unclean food.

Surprisingly, we find fascinating quotations within ancient Jewish literature about Messiah *changing* the kosher laws. This lends credibility to the view that some Jews expected Messiah to change (but not eliminate) the Torah of Moses. Consider the expectations of some rabbis who lived admittedly after the time of Jesus, but may have expressed earlier views.

Midrash Tehillim, commenting on Psalm146:7, states,

> The Lord allows the forbidden ... and will one day allow the eating of all animals now forbidden to be eaten ... In the time to come he will allow every thing that he has forbidden.

In *Lev. Rabbah 13:3* we read, "A new Torah shall go forth from me." *Yalkut* in regard to Isaiah 26:2 says, "the messiah himself will teach it" (the new Torah).[62]

Whether Jesus' words give Messianic Jews freedom to eat non-kosher food is a matter of debate within that community – and beyond the scope of this book. Whatever is unclear should be debated, but the clear is obvious: Yeshua ruled that our hearts' condition and response toward God is a greater priority than the dietary restrictions of Deuteronomy.

> *Food, Jewish Laws and Gentile Believers*

The ruling of the Jerusalem Council in Acts 15:19-21 is straightforward. Gentile believers in Yeshua did not need to submit to circumcision or follow the Jewish laws in

---
[62]"The Law of Moses is Eternal," http://hadavar.org/drupal/content/law-moses-eternal

order to be saved – or in order to fellowship with the Messianic community. Later portions of the *Second Testament* add that gentile believers were not required to observe the Sabbath Day. This is consistent with frequent rabbinic teaching about "alien believers," gentiles who turned from their sins and embraced the God of Israel by faith. Although these "alien believers" were not full converts to Judaism, rabbis associated with *Bet Hillel* considered these gentiles to be heirs of eternal life (we will expand on this subject and document these beliefs later in this book). Attached to their faith was the responsibility to follow the Noahide commandments (cf. Genesis 9:3-7).

The Noahide commandments were extrapolated from the contract between God and Noah's descendents (thus all mankind). The simple restrictions placed upon gentile believers in Yeshua (Acts 15) were probably the enforcement of these Noahide commands. Thus, the Jerusalem Council was embracing the philosophy of the rabbis from *Bet Hillel* who set the Noahide commands as the standard for saved gentiles. Since first century Judaism was certainly not a coherent belief system (beyond a few essentials), we can observe within the Jerusalem Council a debate that predated Christianity.[63] A gentile might ally himself with Judaism at a variety of levels. A *pagan* (unbeliever) would probably be an idolater or one who worships many gods, not serving

---

[63] *Volume One* of the great two-part study, *Justification and Variegated Nomism*, edited by D.A. Carson, Peter T. O'Brien, and Mark A. Seifred; this work goes into great length to evidence the diversity of views regarding salvation during Second Temple Judaism. This refutes the view of Sanders and the *New Perspective* movement by disproving their assumption of a cohesive "Covenantal Nomism."

the true God Yahweh – and thus lost; an *alien believer* would be a gentile who wanted to be saved, repented from his sins and turned to the God of Israel in faith; he was expected to abide by the *Noahide commands* (listed below). A *God-fearer* was an *alien believer* who also observed the Sabbath, abided by the dietary laws of Israel, and participated in synagogue training and worship. A *Jewish convert* (proselyte) was a *God-fearer* who submitted to circumcision and ritual immersion (baptism). He would be expected to provide sacrifices and pay the Temple tax. The lowest standard for any true believer, therefore, was the Noahide commands. The Rabbis derived the following rules from the Covenant of Noah: (1) no idolatry, (2) no incest/adultery, (3) no murder, (4) no blasphemy (profaning God's Name), (5) no theft, (6) justice toward others, and (7) no eating flesh with blood in it and/or cutting off flesh from a living animal.[64]

Summary and Implications

By developing the aforementioned texts in Deuteronomy, Yeshua's verdict is that man's problem is within his heart. Rather than being inclined toward God, it is inclined toward self-gratification. The issues that matter most are neither external nor ritualistic ones (not even kosher laws), but internal issues based upon heart attitudes.

The clear implication is that our sin struggles are really heart issues, and we must therefore seek internal solutions for internal problems. This theme is developed throughout the *Second Testament*. Perhaps Paul's clarity resonates with the western mind:

---

[64]Fischer, John, editor, *The Enduring Paradox: Exploratory Essays in Messianic Judaism*, pp. 176-178.

"Those who live according to the sinful nature have their minds set on what that nature desires; but those who live in accordance with the Spirit have their minds set on what the Spirit desires" (Romans 8:5).

Setting one's mind on the "things of the Spirit" bears similarity to the Old Testament and Jewish concept of renewing the mind through absorption with the Torah. This theme dominates the Bible's longest chapter, Psalm 119. The *Talmud* reflects a similar thought,

> Blessed is Israel; when they occupy themselves with Torah and acts of kindness their inclination is mastered by them, not they by their inclination.[65]

David himself built upon this concept in Psalm 86:11, when he prayed "give me an undivided heart." Followers of Yeshua frequently echo David's desire.

At night, the Jewish people were taught by oral tradition and later the *Talmud* to recite a prayer, part of which included,

> …and bring me not into sin, or into iniquity, or into temptation, or into contempt. And may the good inclination have sway over me and let not the evil inclination have sway over me.[66]

The lessons are clear: those of us who have a saving relationship with Jesus Christ are still sinners within; but God has also given us a new nature, another "kidney." We will not be free of temptation and will still sin until we are perfected in glory. But the simple

---

[65] *Abodah Zarah*, 5b
[66] *Berakoth* 60b

promise holds: if we set our minds on the things of the Spirit, we will not carry out the works of the flesh.[67]

---

[67]See Galatians 5:16ff

Chapter 3: Midrashim on the Mount, Part One: *Light, Divorce, Vows (*Deuteronomy 4:5-8 and Matthew 5:14-16; Deuteronomy 24:1-4 and Matthew 19:7-9; Deuteronomy 23:21-23 and Matthew 5:33-37)

Introduction: Approaching the Sermon on the Mount

I provided readers a sneak preview of our desire to better understand *The Sermon on the Mount (*abbreviated *"SOM")* through *The Midrash Key* in Chapter One. Yeshua's teachings within this sermon may seem to contradict some of his own teachings, as well as lessons from The Book of Acts, the Epistles, and the *First Testament*.

Because we have removed Yeshua from his rabbinic, first century Jewish context, we are plagued with discrepancies. Once we restore Jesus' words to their social, theological, and cultural context, our problem generally fades away. For nearly two millennia, *paradigm blindness* has kept us from perceiving some of Jesus' teachings as rabbinic. By use of *Midrash* and familiarity with the Jewish debates of the day, we can increase the context and better understand the meaning of his words.

➤ *Three Assertions About the Relationship Between The SOM and the Torah*

Commentators have rightly compared the *SOM* to the time Moses presented the Torah to the people. Both addresses were delivered from mountaintops; both were directed toward a massive crowd; both bore the aura of authority. But beyond these convergences, I would like to call into question a few common assumptions and offer alternatives.

First, Yeshua is NOT delivering a "New Law" and thus eliminating the Law of Moses. He is interpreting and applying the Mosaic Torah. If such is the case, then seeking out the initial Torah text follows logically. Finding this text increases overall context.

Second, as pointed out previously, many of Jesus' teachings are rabbinic "fences," intended to provide a protective barrier for the 613 *mitzvot* of the Torah. I propose that *the original Torah laws should still be the focus. We should view Yeshua as "fine-tuning" those commands via fences.*[68] We must recognize that Jesus is building upon a Torah text, not eliminating it.

Since Christians follow Yeshua as Lord, Savior, and Rabbi, they are obligated to observe his fences. Thus the *SOM* can be considered additional Torah.[69] When it comes to interpretation, we can only properly understand the fences in light of the Torah commands they protect.

Fences are limited in perimeter; they only guard a *mitzvah* from certain angles. For example, it is possible to murder without hating the victim. Nonetheless, Yeshua's ruling

---

[68] We should view the *Second Testament* not as a replacement of the First, but rather as a honing and adapting of the First.

[69] The word "Torah" means "instruction" and thus not necessarily limited to the Books of Moses. When I say that Jesus' words are not the "New Law," I mean that his teachings were not intended to replace the Torah.

against hatred addresses most instances in which murder might be a temptation; this safeguard precludes the most common violation of the *mitzvah*.

Third, Yeshua participated in the Torah debates of the day. If we can discover what these controversies were, we can further increase context. What were the rabbis arguing about? What were the hot potatoes of the era?

> *The Nature of The Written Record of The SOM*

If we read *The Sermon on the Mount* aloud, it would take approximately 11 minutes. Christ probably spoke 3 to 4 hours, but even if he spoke as little as two hours, where is the full text? This leads us to an obvious conclusion: the words we have in the Gospels are summary highlights.

While there are obvious patterns to the synoptics (Matthew, Mark, and Luke), the Bible student soon realizes that the Gospel writers took a casual approach toward chronological sequence as well.[70] Thus we cannot be sure that the portion of the *SOM* we read is actually sequential, and we cannot know what was left out in the Biblical record. When it comes to matters like summaries, etc., we must remind ourselves that the Scriptures are arranged by God's Spirit moving upon human authors, no matter what the mechanics.[71]

---

[70] Compare the two accounts of Jesus' temptation in the wilderness (Matthew 4:1-11 and Luke 4:1-13) to see an example of this. Note the order of temptations differs. It is unfair to take the modern obsession with exact chronology and force it upon ancient cultures. When a text purports an exact chronology, we can accept it as such. When an exact chronology is not promised, we have no reason to expect it. Presentations need not be chronologically detailed to be orderly.

[71] See 2 Peter 1:21.

Amazingly, when I seek out the "mother text" passages in the *First Testament*, I come across instances where the Gospel subject matter follows the order of Torah subject matter. Such phenomenon validates our belief that Yeshua often used *Midrash* and taught through a text, at least sometimes. The *SOM* is an orderly collection of *Midrashic* distillations, illustrations, and fences. This is exactly what we would expect from *Midrashim*.

> ➢ *The SOM: Collection from Repeated Deliveries*

The Sermon on the Mount was delivered on a **mount**, according to Matthew 5:1. It is recorded for us in greatest detail in Matthew 5-7. Chapter 6 of Luke's Gospel tenders similar material, but in Luke's account, Yeshua is preaching the *Sermon on the* ***Plain***. Like modern Christian conference speakers, Christ repeated similar teaching to differing crowds. Thus the words recorded in Matthew 5-7 were probably repeated in a variety of arrangements, with spontaneous additions and deletions – and on a number of occasions. The teaching of the *SOM* – whether delivered on hills, plains, shorelines or boats – is our primary concern.

Although I cannot exegete the entire *SOM* in a few chapters, I hope to demonstrate how *The Midrash Key* can be used to increase context and understanding. As already mentioned, the key book for the *SOM* is Deuteronomy.[72]

Yeshua simplifies the principles behind these Deuteronomy passages to make them "hands on," readily accessible for daily life. Rabbinic summations made *mitzvot* user-friendly, but *they were never intended to replace the more detailed teaching of the Torah*. Both Jesus' words[73] and the Torah[74] will never be destroyed; the Scriptures teach that there is *a sense* in which the Law has passed away, yet there is another sense in which it is eternal and relevant.[75]

Midrash One: This Little Light of Mine

The first principle for our consideration is simple to grasp: Yeshua expects his followers to shine as God's lights in a dark world. Our correlated texts consist of Deuteronomy 4:5-8 and Matthew 5:14-16. Let's begin with the Deuteronomy text:

> See, I have taught you decrees and laws as the LORD my God commanded me, so that you may follow them in the land you are entering to take possession of it.

---

[72] I especially appreciated a brief paper by Richard Lee titled, *The Teaching of Jesus from Deuteronomy* [source: http://www.schoolofministry.org.uk/Admin/Content/Resources/Teaching%20of%20Jesus%20from%20Deuteronomy.pdf] accessed 11-16-09.
Once one embraces the theory that many of Jesus' teachings find their origin in Deuteronomy, it is amazing what the Biblically fluent Christian can detect through a casual listening and read through Deuteronomy!
[73] See Matthew 24:35.
[74] See Matthew 5:17.
[75] Many passages teach the relevance of *all* Scripture, such as 2 Timothy 3:16-17, and the Torah's enduring relevance, such as Deuteronomy 29:29 ("forever"). Note Psalm 119:152, "Long ago I learned from your statutes that you established them to last forever." Although Paul argues that the Law was in some sense temporary (Galatians 3:23-25), it seems evident that it is also in some sense eternal.

Observe them carefully, for this will show your wisdom and understanding to the nations, who will hear about all these decrees and say, "Surely this great nation is a wise and understanding people." What other nation is so great as to have their gods near them the way the LORD our God is near us whenever we pray to him? And what other nation is so great as to have such righteous decrees and laws as this body of laws I am setting before you today?

> *Living to Impress Others with Yahweh*

If the Jewish people reverently observed the decrees of the Torah, other nations would marvel and recognize Yahweh as both (1) the giver of Torah and (2) the one who is in unique relationship with Israel. The pagans would be *impressed* with Yahweh.

Both Israel and the church share the same purpose: to glorify God. Although we may glorify our Lord in a number of ways, one significant way is to impress the heathen with Yahweh's glory by reflecting his light. Thus even the unbeliever finds himself ascribing majesty to the Creator!

Do not confuse this with the *conversion* of the heathen. Other texts assert that God is glorified when sinners repent, but Yahweh is glorified in a different way when unconverted sinners praise Him.[76]

King Nebuchadnezzar is a prime example. In Daniel 4, God warned that he would humble Nebuchadnezzar if he did not humble himself. Nebuchadnezzar ignored the warning and was disciplined by God. For seven years he thought he was an animal and grazed among the livestock. When his sanity returned, Nebuchadnezzar was impressed

---

[76] Psalm 66:3 speaks of God's enemies "cringing" (NASB) or "feigning obedience" (ASV) before him during the Kingdom age. They are still God's enemies, but their obedience brings the Lord glory.

with Yahweh's ability to humble the proud. He worshiped and acknowledged the "God of heaven;" he sent out a circular letter exalting God throughout his kingdom; *yet he still continued in his pagan worship.*

- *Yeshua's Distillation*

Let's peruse Matthew 5:14-16 and then correlate the two passages:

> "You are the light of the world. A city on a hill cannot be hidden. Neither do people light a lamp and put it under a bowl. Instead they put it on its stand, and it gives light to everyone in the house. In the same way, let your light shine before men, that they may see your good deeds and praise your Father in heaven."

In Matthew, Yeshua illustrates the points made in Deuteronomy in *Midrashic* style: he uses stories, imagery, or parables. In this case, we can detect a difference between the Deuteronomy passage and the Matthew passage. In Deuteronomy, the focus is the *collective* nation. In Matthew, the focus is the *individual* – the godly from among the people, particularly Jesus' disciples.

The individual believer is like a bright light that should be set on a hill for all to see. He then summarizes how to do this: our good deeds will so impress "men" (meaning "men outside the group") that they would glorify the Father in heaven. Note the text does not promise that such "men" would necessarily join the ranks of Christ's disciples.

Paul might be presenting a similar *Midrash* of his own in I Corinthians 14:23-25:

> So if the whole church comes together and everyone speaks in tongues, and some who do not understand or some unbelievers come in, will they not say that you are out of your mind? But if an unbeliever or someone who does not understand comes in

while everybody is prophesying, he will be convinced by all that he is a sinner and will be judged by all, and the secrets of his heart will be laid bare. So he will fall down and worship God, exclaiming, "God is really among you!"

Here believers are likewise trying to impress an unbeliever; whether or not this guest will become a convert is not stated. If he remains unconverted, he might be an "impressed" unbeliever, like Nebuchadnezzar. Evangelism and discipleship are crucial elements in the church's attempt to glorify God, but not the only elements.

Yeshua adapts the Deuteronomy passage to address the present realities and needs of the times. Because Jesus' church is made up of individual believers, the call to good works must be directed toward the individual. Contrast this with Deuteronomy, in which God is covenanting with the entire Israelite nation. Yeshua is drawing those who have a heightened spiritual appetite, a spiritual appetite he defines in the beatitudes. If Yeshua's disciples could multiply themselves, perhaps the nation would repent and the Messianic Kingdom would begin.[77]

> *Religious Diversity Among the Jews*

---

[77] Even as late as Acts 3:19-21, the offer is made to the nation that, if they repented and would turn to Jesus, the Kingdom (The Promised Millennium) would soon follow: "Repent, then, and turn to God, so that your sins may be wiped out, that times of refreshing may come from the Lord, and *that he may send the Christ*, who has been appointed for you—even Jesus. He must remain in heaven until the time comes for God to restore everything, as he promised long ago through his holy prophets." This is not to say that the present course of events was unanticipated by God.

During the time of Yeshua's ministry, Israel's religious beliefs were diverse and sometimes compromised. As the *Jerusalem Talmud* states, "Israel went into exile only after it became divided into twenty-four sects." [78]

Rather than the nation being absorbed with God's Torah and shining the light, some Jews were quite devout while many others were far from devout. Apart from the essentials of Judaism (the oneness of God, refraining from idolatry, the truth of the Torah, etc.), Israel's belief system was a patchwork. The Dead Sea Scroll people, the Essenes, considered Temple worship so defiled that they criticized it sharply; some suggest that the Essenes did not participate in it, while some suggest otherwise.[79] The Sadducees – the theological liberals of their day – generally did not believe in the entire *Tanakh* (i.e., Old Testament) but only accepted the Torah; most denied the afterlife, angels and demons. The Sadducees were the rich, powerful, and corrupt families who controlled the high priesthood. The Pharisees were made up of some very devout individuals, but some of the most politically influential Pharisees were corrupt and Pharisees in name only. We have previously discussed the two main Pharisaical divisions, *Bet Shammai* and *Bet Hillel*.

---

[78] *Jerusalem Talmud, Sanhedrin 29C,* quoted by William C.Varner in *"Jesus and the Pharisees,"* www.pfo.org/pharisee.htm.

[79] The Essenes considered atonement and salvation to be independent of the Jewish Temple and priesthood, by some interpretations. See D.A. Carson (editor), *Justification and Variegated Nomism, Volume 1*, pp. pp. 382-414, esp. p. 401. Contrasting Jesus to the Essenes, Anne Punton comments, "The Essenes held aloof from Temple life, Jesus did not," *The World Jesus Knew*, p. 248. J. Dwight Pentecost tells us that, "They did not go to the Temple but sent their tribute," *The Words and Works of Jesus Christ*, p. 542. Not everyone, however, accepts this viewpoint. Falk argues that the Essenes were directly connected to *Bet Hillel* and that many functioning priests *were* Essenes. See Harvey Falk, *Jesus the Pharisee*, pp. 39-62.

The *Talmud* mostly represents the mainstream viewpoints of *Bet Hillel*. Members of *Bet Hillel* typically rebuked the flaws of fellow Pharisees. Thus Yeshua's harsh condemnation of the Pharisees should not be understood as unusual: he was embracing the Hillel tradition of calling for reform, repentance, and self-examination, beginning with the most religious.[80] Christ was not writing off the Pharisees – as might easily be misunderstood from the Gospel accounts. Will Varner summarizes a number of Talmudic passages – written by Pharisees associated with *Bet Hillel* – that categorize the integrity level of various Pharisees:

> There is a passage, appearing in slightly different forms in both the *Babylonian* and *Jerusalem Talmuds*. This passage sheds light on the self-perception of the Pharisees. This passage describes seven different types of Pharisees. A paraphrase of the difficult Talmudic language describes the following seven: (1) The "shoulder" Pharisee wore his good deeds on his shoulder so everyone could see them. (2) The "wait a little" Pharisee always found an excuse for putting off a good deed. (3) The "bruised" Pharisee shut his eyes to avoid seeing a woman and knocked into walls, bruising himself. (4) The "humpbacked" Pharisee always walked bent double, in false humility. (5) The "ever reckoning" Pharisee was always counting up the numbers of his good deeds. (6) The "fearful" Pharisee always quaked in fear of the wrath of God. (7) The "God-loving" Pharisee was a copy of Abraham who lived in faith and charity.[81]

---

[80] They very much embraced the attitude of I Peter 4:17-18, "For it is time for judgment to begin with the family of God; and if it begins with us, what will the outcome be for those who do not obey the gospel of God? And, 'If it is hard for the righteous to be saved,
what will become of the ungodly and the sinner?'"
[81] William C. Varner, *Jesus and the Pharisees: A Jewish Perspective,* http://www.pfo.org/pharisee.htm, accessed 11-18-09.

Other Jews belonged to the terrorist group we refer to as "The Zealots"[82] while yet others – designated as "Herodians" – had adopted Greek culture and sometimes gentile values. Grecian Jews filled the Mediterranean world; while many Grecian Jews were devout, others made significant compromises with the cultures of their new homelands.[83] Yeshua's disciples represented some of this diversity. Whereas Peter, Andrew, and Nathaniel were devout Torah students, Matthew Levi had compromised by serving as a tax-collector for the Romans. Simon the Zealot had been part of the notorious Jewish terrorist group.

> *Application*

According to the *Tanakh*, the main mechanism for godly growth was Torah study and meditation upon the Scriptures.[84] Students were challenged to do God's will, not just read and study. Yet they understood that discovering God's will is connected to reading, studying, and becoming fluent in the Scriptures. One cannot worship God without diligently studying his Word. Abraham Joshua Heschel captures the crux:

> "....while the Greeks studied to comprehend and Western thinkers study to apply knowledge in a practical sense, the ancient Hebrews studied to revere."[85]

Midrash Two: Divorce and Remarriage

---

[82] Simon the Zealot, one of Jesus' disciples, had this background. Dwight Pentecost (*The Words and Works of Jesus Christ*, p. 542) comments, "The Zealots…insisted on war against Rome." He then points out that they agitated the rebellion that resulted in the destruction of Jerusalem in 70 A.D.
[83] H. W. Hoehner's article in *The International Standard Bible Encyclopedia, Volume 2*, p. 698, does a fine job of postulating the nature of the Herodians.
[84] Psalm 1 and Psalm 119 underscore this belief.
[85] Brad H. Young, *Jesus, The Jewish Theologian*, p.266.

> *Yahweh, A God of Well-placed Concessions*

My presentation of this *Midrash* is colored by my viewpoints about the Biblical teaching regarding the controversial subject of divorce. Please understand my thoughts as one possible understanding of this issue from a Jewish Roots perspective.

The Torah is an interwoven, complicated mesh; it contains revelations describing God's specified will, theology, religious ritual, rulings about justice, clarifications about what is and what is not sin, and principles for governing a theocratic nation. Some might be surprised to learn that the Torah also includes a number of divine *concessions*. The realities of sinful human nature require a gracious God to make provision for failure. As we read the Bible narratives, we can note that God sometimes makes concessions.[86]

In our texts, we see: (1) God's regulation of divorce, and (2) Yeshua's attempt to distinguish between God's concession and God's ideal. Yahweh's concession is divorce, but his ideal is lifelong marriage.

Deuteronomy 24:1-4 (NASB) reads,

> When a man takes a wife and marries her, and it happens that she finds no favor in his eyes because he has found some indecency in her, and he writes her a certificate of divorce and puts it in her hand and sends her out from his house, and she leaves his house and goes and becomes another man's wife, and if the latter husband turns against her and writes her a certificate of divorce and puts it in her hand and sends her out of his house, or if the latter husband dies who took her to be his wife, then her

---

[86] The examples of Moses (Exodus 4:10-16) and Gideon (Judges 6:36-40) are two simple illustrations of concession. Psalm 103:13-14 exemplify God's disposition toward us: "As a father has compassion on his children, so the LORD has compassion on those who fear him; for he knows how we are formed, he remembers that we are dust."

former husband who sent her away is not allowed to take her again to be his wife, since she has been defiled; for that is an abomination before the LORD, and you shall not bring sin on the land which the LORD your God gives you as an inheritance.

Note that this text nowhere demands divorce, but allows for it when a man finds "some indecency" in his wife. If a man chooses to pursue a divorce in such a case, he must make the divorce official by writing a certificate of divorce. If the wife should choose to marry another, she may never return to her first husband.

The ancient sages debated this question: What is the meaning of the phrase, "some indecency?" Modern Christians also struggle with these and related issues. This text could raise many, many questions. For example, do the restrictions about remarrying a former spouse apply to the New Covenant believer? Should a believer marry an idolater who has fathered her child? Can one divorce for a variety of reasons if he remains unmarried? Unfortunately, must limit our discussion to the main question.

Second Temple Jewish leaders did not agree about what the phrase, "some indecency" meant. The *Talmud* captures the debate between the two major competing rabbinic schools, *Bet Hillel* and *Bet Shammai*:

> The house of Shammai say, a man may not put away his wife, unless he finds some uncleanness in her, according to Deu. 24:1. The house of Hillel say, if she should spoil his food, (that is, as Jarchi and Bartenora explain it, burns it either at the fire, or with salt, i.e. over-roasts or over-salts it,) who appeal also to Deu. 24:1. R. Akiba says, if he finds another more beautiful than her, as it is said, Deu. 24:1 "and it come to pass that she find no favour in his eyes."[87]

---

[87] *Mishnah Gittin, 9.10.*

Shammai's position was understood as referring to marital unfaithfulness. Hillel's position – the one adopted by most modern Jews – was that a man could divorce his wife for any reason. Jesus – who typically sided with *Bet Hillel* – broke rank with Hillel on this matter and embraced the view of *Bet Shammai*. Although Yeshua mostly experienced conflict with *Bet Shammai*, he was not afraid to step on the toes of *Bet Hillel* either.[88]

➢ *The Matter of Adultery*

Since the *First Testament* penalty for adultery was death, why would Yahweh make provision for divorce on the basis of adultery? If the death penalty were carried out, divorce would not be necessary (in most instances).[89]

Matters are not that simple. From a practical viewpoint, adultery had to be legally provable. If proven, then *both* offending parties were to be stoned.[90]

When Israel was under the dominion of another empire (Persian, Roman, etc.), she was not free to do as God commanded. But even when the Torah could be fully obeyed, it seemed the Jewish people preferred to err on the side of grace. Jewish teachers avoided

---

[88] This viewpoint cannot be proven, but the evidence for such an assertion is the topics of debate between Jesus and some of the Pharisees. Since the *Bet Hillel* was much more humane and flexible in comparison with the rigid, trite *Bet Shammai* (especially over matters like the Sabbath, washing of hands, tithing, etc.); my proposal is that terms like "the Pharisees" and "the Jews" refer to specific groups from the larger groups. In other words, "the Pharisees" refers to part of the Pharisees, namely the more influential *Bet Shammai*. I am not suggesting that Pharisees from the *Bet Hillel* never opposed Jesus. I am suggesting that most of Christ's *theological opposition* came from the *Bet Shammai*. Perhaps the "non-disciple" exorcist referenced in Mark 9:38-39 was from *Bet Hillel*?

[89] Most understand the term "immorality" to refer to adultery and other perversions (or even flirtations). It includes – but is not necessarily limited to – adultery.

[90] The question raised in the story of the "woman taken in adultery" (John 8:3-11) is, "Where is the man?"

the harsh penalties of the Torah by making prosecution tedious or demanding monetary equivalencies in place of retribution. The conditions that needed to be met and technical evasions made capital punishment a rare event.[91] In this way, Jewish authorities could claim to obey Torah while negating the less desirable *mitzvot*.

To complicate matters, God himself set a confusing example when he chose to demonstrate grace rather than justice on a number of occasions. David's adultery with Bathsheba – and the murder he arranged in his attempt to hush up his adultery – offers a case study. The nature of David's sins demanded he be put to death, according to a straightforward understanding of Torah.[92] But God nowhere demanded this penalty be exacted, despite the fact that Yahweh himself had dictated the Torah laws. These facts are puzzling, but the simplest explanation is that God is free to be as gracious as he chooses to be.

> *God's Desire for Marriage: Lifelong*

What was Yeshua's reason for siding with the *Bet Shammai* on this issue? Jesus' logic is amplified in Matthew 19:7-9,

---

[91] For example, the rabbis avoiding stoning rebellious sons by creating a technical definition as to how rebellion is defined. The Babylonian *Talmud* reads, "If he stole of his father's and ate it in his father's domain, or of strangers and ate it in the domain of strangers, or of strangers and ate in his father's domain, he does not become a 'stubborn and rebellious son' — until he steals of his father's and eats in the domain of strangers. R. Jose, son of R. Judah said: until he steals of his father's and mother's [*Sanhedrin, Folio 71a*]." This sort of evasive interpretation is common in the *Talmud*.

[92] Leviticus 20:10 reads, " 'If a man commits adultery with another man's wife—with the wife of his neighbor—both the adulterer and the adulteress must be put to death.'"

> "Why then," they asked, "did Moses command that a man give his wife a certificate of divorce and send her away?"
>
> Jesus replied, "Moses permitted you to divorce your wives because your hearts were hard. But it was not this way from the beginning. I tell you that anyone who divorces his wife, except for marital unfaithfulness, and marries another woman commits adultery."

Christ's reasoning is as follows: God created marriage in Eden. God took the woman from the man. Just as Eve was taken from Adam's side, so in marriage Eve returns to Adam's side – Adam and Eve are once again one flesh.

Divorce was added in the Torah as a concession to human sinfulness, a necessity in some situations because of a fallen world. But marital dissolution was not God's original intent. The less-detailed account of Mark 10:11-12 suggests that Jesus extends the same standards to both genders.

> ➢ *Paul Addresses A Divorce Issue Yeshua Did Not Address*

We do not know *all* that Jesus said about the subject of divorce, and we would do well to remember that. Yet we do know one area he did not address: a believer deserted by an unbeliever. Paul seems to quote Jesus, setting the tone for the Christian's overall perspective on matters of divorce and remarriage. After quoting Jesus, Paul then indicates that he is addressing a divorce issue Jesus never spoke about. Note this passage from I Corinthians 7:10-15, *passim*:

> To the married I give this command (not I, but the Lord): A wife must not separate from her husband. But if she does, she must remain unmarried or else be reconciled to her husband. And a husband must not divorce his wife…

> To the rest I say this (I, not the Lord): If any brother has a wife who is not a believer and she is willing to live with him, he must not divorce her. And if a woman has a husband who is not a believer and he is willing to live with her, she must not divorce him. …But if the unbeliever leaves, let him do so. A believing man or woman is not bound in such circumstances; God has called us to live in peace.

Paul quotes the Lord by saying "not I, but the Lord" and then adds, "To the rest I say this (I, not the Lord)." Paul is not implying that his own words are uninspired or non-authoritative; he is saying that Christ never touched upon this particular situation.

> *Implications*

Many of Jesus' statements express general, broad-brush principles; not all are finely nuanced teachings applicable to all situations. They are frequently partial truths, not whole truths. When Yeshua wanted to make a "no exceptions" statement, he was capable of doing so, as he did in John 14:6, for example.[93]

Still, we must note that Jesus' teaching on divorce and remarriage seems more than a mere fence. What we have is a firm ruling – a dogmatic interpretation of Scripture. This moves beyond mere rabbinic debate, for the one teaching (Messiah) is not merely an ordinary rabbi. We can be sure that the exception clause in Deuteronomy, "something indecent," does not refer to something trite, like a wife burning her husband's dinner. Although the Messiah's words carry great weight, we should not read more into them than Yeshua said. Nowhere is a wrongful divorce and remarriage designated as an

---

[93] Jesus answered, "I am the way and the truth and the life. No one comes to the Father except through me."

unpardonable sin. Yet, at the same time, such a sin may disqualify one from certain levels of spiritual leadership.[94]

Although we might interpret ancient Judaism as embracing overly-permissive views regarding divorce, most ancient Jewish values supported the family. The rabbis encouraged men to love their wives as they loved themselves, a viewpoint familiar to most Christians.[95] One *Talmud* excerpt reads:

> Our Rabbis taught: Concerning a man who loves his wife as himself, who honours her more than himself, who guides his sons and daughters in the right path and arranges for them to be married … Scripture says, "And thou shalt know that thy tent is in peace." [96]

Midrash Three: Vows

Jesus builds a fence to help us avoid misusing God's Name by misusing vows. Our correlated texts are Deuteronomy 23:21-23 and Matthew 5:33-37.

Deuteronomy 23:21-23 reads:

> If you make a vow to the LORD your God, do not be slow to pay it, for the LORD your God will certainly demand it of you and you will be guilty of sin. But if you refrain from making a vow, you will not be guilty. Whatever your lips utter you must be sure to do, because you made your vow freely to the LORD your God with your own mouth.

Jesus builds the protective fence in Matthew 5:33-37:

---

[94] In I Timothy 3, we can find several phrases that may be construed to limit candidates for elder (vs. 2) or deacon (vs. 12) who have been divorced (at least in some instances).
[95] Ephesians 5:25-28, esp. 28b, "…He who loves his wife loves himself."
[96] *Yebamoth 62*

> "Again, you have heard that it was said to the people long ago, 'Do not break your oath, but keep the oaths you have made to the Lord.' But I tell you, Do not swear at all: either by heaven, for it is God's throne; or by the earth, for it is his footstool; or by Jerusalem, for it is the city of the Great King. And do not swear by your head, for you cannot make even one hair white or black. Simply let your 'Yes' be 'Yes,' and your 'No,' 'No'; anything beyond this comes from the evil one."

The Torah declares that making a vow to God was a serious matter because God expected his people to follow through. The Deuteronomy text tells us that vows were *not required*.

➢ *Weaseling Out of Vows Through Technicalities*

In Matthew, Yeshua addresses an apparently rampant problem. The text itself suggests that some Jews were weaseling out of their vows by finding technical loopholes. The argument seemed to be that since they had not pronounced God's Name while making the vows, they were free to break them.

Ancient and modern Jews refrained from pronouncing God's name, "Yahweh," (LORD) and sparingly used his titles like Adonai (Lord) or Elohim (God);[97] they would swear by heaven, earth, Jerusalem, or their own name. Whether Yeshua approved of these fences or not, he condemned the entire loophole concept. They had taken a rabbinic fence and used that fence to circumvent the true requirement of the *mitzvah*.

Since vows were not required in the Torah, Christ advises his disciples to avoid the sordid mess by refusing to make vows in the first place. Simple honesty precludes the necessity of making vows while humbly allowing for the unforeseen.

---

[97] Many Jews would use terms like, "Ha Shem" – meaning, "The Name" or "The Holy One – Blessed is He!" when referring to God.

Solomon did not go quite as far as Yeshua, but he did write in Ecclesiastes 5:4-6,

> When you make a vow to God, do not delay in fulfilling it. He has no pleasure in fools; fulfill your vow. It is better not to vow than to make a vow and not fulfill it. Do not let your mouth lead you into sin. And do not protest to the temple messenger, "My vow was a mistake." Why should God be angry at what you say and destroy the work of your hands?

> ➤ *A Better Fence*

Jesus' advice – to avoid making vows – is a fence around the Torah command. Yeshua's words should not be inflated to imply that we should balk at required vows – as taking an oath in court or making vows at the marriage altar, for example. The fence exists to protect the commandment, and offers a practical way to do so. It is not morally wrong to make a vow, but why risk an infraction if the risk serves no real purpose?

Conclusion

We have looked briefly at three *Midrashim* found in the *SOM*. By using *The Midrash Key*, we can now better understand: what it means to be a light in dark world, the whys and wherefores of divorce, and the importance of maintaining personal integrity by refusing to make spurious vows.

Chapter 4: Midrashim on the Mount, Part Two: Materialism, Riches, and God's Provision
(Deuteronomy 8:3-18, Matthew 6:24-34, Matthew 19:22-26)

I have been preaching for over 30 years, but when I prepared a sermon coupling the first two passages cited above, I was overwhelmed. My outline for the Deuteronomy 8 passage and my outline for Matthew 6 were virtually identical. I felt as though I had uncovered a hidden treasure that had been buried for two millennia. This Deuteronomy passage must be the text Yeshua used as the basis for a well-known segment of the *SOM*.

Jesus' Teachings About Money

> *Easily Misunderstood*

Both layman and theologian can completely misunderstand Yeshua's teaching about material needs and wealth. We commonly hear assertions like, "Jesus taught that rich men cannot go to heaven, but poor people are the children of God." Certain cults and religious orders exalt poverty while condemning wealth, as though poverty were a virtue and wealth a great evil. On the other extreme, "prosperity" teachers claim that God wants everyone to be wealthy and comfortable. How can we account for such extreme differences of interpretation?

Reading Jesus' words alone – apart from broader context – *could* lead us to either of these extreme conclusions. Such conclusions, however, contradict the *First Testament* and the rest of the *Second Testament*.[98] We should therefore be suspicious about both extremes.

Whenever we are asked to "play" Christ against the Torah, the prophets, or the apostles, something is amuck. If *all* Scripture is equally inspired, we cannot entertain the idea that Christ contradicts Paul or Moses. A Bible divided cannot stand.

If we broaden our context through *Midrash* and understand the issues of the era, Yeshua's teachings take on a less radical meaning and harmonize perfectly with the rest of God's Word.[99]

Like other rabbis, Yeshua frequently focuses upon certain threads of truth, not necessarily the entire rope. We might consider his teachings a single gem from the multi-stringed necklace of truth. We need to alert ourselves to the difference between truth and whole truth.

We will depart for our excursion from Station Deuteronomy, and then travel with the Messiah to our new destination, Station Matthew.

---

[98] Ben Witherington, in his work, *The Acts of the Apostles*, offers a rabbit-trail article titled, "A Closer Look– The Social Status and Level of the Earliest Christians," on pages 210-213. On page 212, he concludes, "Thus there were some who were reasonably well off, though probably not among the wealthiest elite." In I Timothy 6:17-19, Paul does not advise the rich to become poor, but rather, "Command those who are rich in this present world not to be arrogant nor to put their hope in wealth, which is so uncertain, but to put their hope in God, who richly provides us with everything for our enjoyment. Command them to do good, to be rich in good deeds, and to be generous and willing to share. In this way they will lay up treasure for themselves as a firm foundation for the coming age, so that they may take hold of the life that is truly life." Riches are not evil, but present the potential danger distracting one from "life that is truly life." This, I believe, is also Jesus' point.

[99] Some have an agenda to make Jesus more radical than he actually was; our goal should be to *understand* Jesus, not use him as ammunition for our particular cause.

Both texts are connected to Israel's 40-year wilderness wandering, beginning with the Exodus. By recalling God's provision during this time, (1) the Israelites in Moses' day could learn some valuable lessons, (2) the Jews in Jesus' time could relearn those same lessons, and (3) believers in any era will develop a better ethic about material goods and money.

> *Our Deuteronomy Text*

The Deuteronomy 8:3-18 lesson distills to this: "Remember God's provision; make God top priority and he will take care of you." Although a long read, it is important that you take the time to do so. After reading this text, see if you agree with my outline summary:

> He humbled you, causing you to hunger and then feeding you with manna, which neither you nor your fathers had known, to teach you that man does not live on bread alone but on every word that comes from the mouth of the LORD.
>
> Your clothes did not wear out and your feet did not swell during these forty years.
>
> Know then in your heart that as a man disciplines his son, so the LORD your God disciplines you. Observe the commands of the LORD your God, walking in his ways and revering him.
>
> For the LORD your God is bringing you into a good land—a land with streams and pools of water, with springs flowing in the valleys and hills; a land with wheat and barley, vines and fig trees, pomegranates, olive oil and honey; a land where bread will not be scarce and you will lack nothing; a land where the rocks are iron and you can dig copper out of the hills.
>
> When you have eaten and are satisfied, praise the LORD your God for the good land he has given you. Be careful that you do not forget the LORD your God, failing to observe his commands, his laws and his decrees that I am giving you this day.
>
> Otherwise, when you eat and are satisfied, when you build fine houses and settle down, and when your herds and flocks grow large and your silver and gold increase and all you have is multiplied, then your heart will become proud and you will forget

the LORD your God, who brought you out of Egypt, out of the land of slavery. He led you through the vast and dreadful desert, that thirsty and waterless land, with its venomous snakes and scorpions. He brought you water out of hard rock. He gave you manna to eat in the desert, something your fathers had never known, to humble and to test you so that in the end it might go well with you.

You may say to yourself, "My power and the strength of my hands have produced this wealth for me." But remember the LORD your God, for it is he who gives you the ability to produce wealth, and so confirms his covenant, which he swore to your forefathers, as it is today.

What did God provide during those long 40 years?

> *Food: Physical and Spiritual*

Yahweh provided them with food, including daily manna and occasional quail. God allowed them to go hungry *first* before he literally showered this food upon them; the reason he allowed them to experience hunger was to develop humility within them.[100] He wanted them to realize how vulnerable they were without God's provision; in addition, he wanted them to appreciate his provision. This delay in providing for them underscored their need to *trust God for daily provision*.

The manna fell *out of the sky*, thus signifying that God provides us daily sustenance. Yeshua builds upon the manna theme with another *Midrash* in John 6:32-34, in which Yeshua suggests that he himself is pictured by the manna.[101]

---

[100] The correlation between hunger and humility is seen in the practice of fasting.
[101] John 6:33-34 (NASB) reads, "Jesus said to them, 'I tell you the truth, it is not Moses who has given you the bread from heaven, but it is my Father who gives you the true bread from heaven. For the bread of God is he who comes down from heaven and gives life to the world.'"

In contrast to many interpreters, I interpret the phrase, "by every Word" to mean that God's Word is the source of our spiritual nurture. This seems to be the obvious, natural meaning.[102] The Lord's provision of the physical – or sometimes his lack of provision – nudges us toward developing a trust relationship with him, and that relationship is mediated through the Scriptures. God's physical provision should draw us to embrace his Word and seek the "other-worldly." We can approach Yahweh to find aid for both the physical and the spiritual. The spiritual exists within and behind the physical.[103] Thus when human needs are met – physical or spiritual – they are met by God's Word. That Word can signify written Scripture or his spoken Word.[104]

Jesus quoted the Scripture, "man shall not live by bread alone" to fend off Satan when the devil tempted him in the wilderness. Both testaments present reading, studying, and memorizing the Word as the primary source for the believer's spiritual nurture.

> *Clothing*

---

[102] Context is king, and the context of Deuteronomy 6 emphatically emphasizes a steady diet of the Torah. Deuteronomy 6:6-9 (KJV) reads, "And these words, which I command thee this day, shall be in thine heart: And thou shalt teach them diligently unto thy children, and shalt talk of them when thou sittest in thine house, and when thou walkest by the way, and when thou liest down, and when thou risest up. And thou shalt bind them for a sign upon thine hand, and they shall be as frontlets between thine eyes. And thou shalt write them upon the posts of thy house, and on thy gates." This sets the tone for Deuteronomy 8.

[103] Philosophically, "realism" often denies the spiritual, "idealism" denies the material, but "representationalism" suggests that the physical exists, but sometimes there is more to what exists than what we can perceive. Behind our daily bread is a God who graciously provides. See *Wikipedia* article on "Direct Realism" for a simple overview, http://en.wikipedia.org/wiki/Common_sense_realism.

[104] Speaking of the Son of God, Hebrews 1:3 reads, "And He is the radiance of His glory and the exact representation of His nature, and **upholds all things by the word** of His power…"

The children of Israel left Egypt with whatever possessions they could carry; no one had anticipated a 40-year detour in the "desert of discipline." Even if they had, how could they stock a 40-year supply of shoes and clothing? Just as God miraculously provided food to feed over two million people per day, so he supernaturally preserved their clothing. To suggest that God's provision of food and clothing was anything but miraculous equates to denying the text. It is not natural for two million homeless people to wander around in the desert for forty years and yet be well fed and well clothed.

> *Looking Back*

The Israelites could glance back at Yahweh's track record. This same God who had provided for them during those 40 years was still at hand – and this same God could continue to provide for his people.

> *Put God First and Enjoy Continued Blessing*

Moses explained that God had disciplined the people as sons. Yahweh did this to motivate them to obey his commands and consequently be blessed in the Promised Land. *If the people would prioritize the Lord and take his commands seriously, this would ensure their long-term prosperity and satisfaction.* In Deuteronomy 8, wealth and prosperity are good things. How can wealth be intrinsically evil if a good God promises it as a reward to an obedient people?

> *The Temptation of Prosperity*

Though wealth is a blessing from the hand of God, sinful men can corrupt this blessing so that it degrades into a curse. Those who are well off may think they no longer *need* God. Prosperous men may conclude that they have produced their own financial success through industry, self-discipline, ability, or personal intelligence. *Affluence can become counter-productive and drive the wealthy away from the God who brought the prosperity.* The Scriptures mention some significant men of wealth who prioritized their walk with God, like Abraham, Job, and some of the godly kings. Others, like Balaam, were ruined by the love of money. The danger is real, because "a full stomach leads to all kinds of sin."[105]

For centuries, the Jews have fought the temptation to forget God by frequently reciting a host of memorized "blessings." Although observant Jews traditionally bless God before meals, the Jewish custom to recite blessings after meals is more emphatic.[106] This is based on Deuteronomy 8:10 (KJV), "When thou hast eaten and art full, then thou shalt bless the LORD thy God for the good land which he hath given thee."[107]

Verse 18a is a key verse toward developing a proper perspective: "But remember the LORD your God, for it is he who gives you the ability to produce wealth..."

---

[105] *Beracot 32a*, quoted from *The Torah Revealed* by Avrahom Yaakov Finkel, p. 283.
[106] Finkel summarized another *Talmud* teaching, "You are required to say Birkat Hamazon after eating a piece of bread the quantity of an olive, according to R. Meir, and the quantity of an egg, according to R. Yehuda (*Berachot 45a*); *The Torah Revealed*, p. 283.
[107] I Timothy 4:4-5 might be a *Midrash* on Deuteronomy 8:10, "For everything created by God is good, and nothing is to be rejected if it is received with gratitude; for it is sanctified by means of the word of God and prayer." The idea here is that food is "set apart" by gratitude toward God.

> *Indirect Provision*

When the children of Israel roamed nomadically in the wilderness, they could neither plant crops nor harvest grain. They simply carried their baskets, picked up the manna that had fallen from the skies, and then cooked it in creative ways. But this longstanding routine was about to change. The simple harvesting of daily manna would be replaced with the demands of agricultural life. The Hebrews would soon be like others: they would plant, cultivate, and reap their own crops. God's provision would become *indirect*. When it came to earthly provision, they were being transferred from the realm of "special grace" to the realm of "common grace."

On the one hand, the wilderness experience demonstrated that God *could* provide and will provide – when it is in his plan to do so. On the other hand, the normal routine of life teaches us not to presume upon God's grace, *but to apply ourselves* toward earning a living.

Seeing God's hand behind our efforts and the cycles of nature is an important Biblical idea. Wayne Grudem refers to this concept as *concurrence*:

> God cooperates with created things in every action, directing their distinctive properties to cause them to act as they do…God directs and works through the distinctive properties of each created thing, so that these things themselves bring about the results we see…[108]

> *Keeping the Commandments: A Way to Honor the Living God*

---

[108] Grudem, Wayne, *Systematic Theology*, pp. 317, 319.

Most of us would never consider surrendering the doctrine of salvation by grace alone through faith alone apart from human merit or good works. If the Scriptures are clear on any point, it is that point.[109]

The Scriptures do maintain that our works are *correlated* with regeneration, even though they do not cause it.[110] Good works are the sure evidence of New Birth. Obedience to God's commands express the regenerate life within, but such obedience cannot create that life.[111]

Since only a small percentage of Bible texts deal with the way of salvation, we must not ignore the main biblical emphasis upon God's glory and our relationship to God. This does not imply that everything in the Bible is other-worldly, for we can glorify God even in the normal routines of life.[112] This is where God's *mitzvot* come into play.

We should not presume that most Jews thought commandment-keeping earned them eternal life, although some did, according to Luke 18:9:

---

[109] The following verses make the point:
Romans 4:4-5, "Now when a man works, his wages are not credited to him as a gift, but as an obligation. However, to the man who does not work but trusts God who justifies the wicked, his faith is credited as righteousness."
Ephesians 2:8-10, "For it is by grace you have been saved, through faith—and this not from yourselves, it is the gift of God— not by works, so that no one can boast. For we are God's workmanship, created in Christ Jesus to do good works, which God prepared in advance for us to do."
Titus 3:4-5, "But when the kindness and love of God our Savior appeared, he saved us, not because of righteous things we had done, but because of his mercy. He saved us through the washing of rebirth and renewal by the Holy Spirit."
[110] Our salvation is judged by our works, but our salvation is not the result of our works. We are rewarded for the works we have done once we are saved; the good works we do before coming into a right relationship with God are like filthy rags. See: Romans 8:1-9, I Corinthians 3:10-15, Isaiah 64:6.
[111] See John 3:1-16.
[112] See I Corinthians 10:31.

> And He also told this parable to some people who trusted in themselves that they were righteous, and viewed others with contempt…

Perhaps most Jews believed they would have "a place in the world to come" simply because they were Jews. John the Baptist refuted this viewpoint, namely, that Jews were saved simply because of physical descent:

> Produce fruit in keeping with repentance. And do not think you can say to yourselves, "We have Abraham as our father." I tell you that out of these stones God can raise up children for Abraham. The ax is already at the root of the trees, and every tree that does not produce good fruit will be cut down and thrown into the fire.[113]

Only apostasy or a life of horrendous ungodliness could disqualify one from life, in some views.[114] Other Jews, such as those in the *Qumran* community, sounded Pauline. They believed in salvation by grace through faith based upon God's election.[115] My point is that many Jews did not view the *mitzvot* as a threatening club of God's wrath. They were generally trying to please God – not appease God – by their obedience.

---

[113] Matthew 3:8-10.

[114] "In the World to Come, Abraham will sit at the entrance to *Gehinom* [the Jewish equivalent to hell] and not allow any circumcised Israelite to descend into it. As for those [Jews] who sinned [and deserve the punishments of Gehinom], what does he do to them? He removes the foreskin from children who had died before circumcision and places it upon them and sends them down to Gehinom!" (Genesis Rabbah 48:8) [cited in an article titled, " Brit Milah: Rabbinic Interpretations" by Rabbi Daniel Kohn. This *Midrash* would have been written several centuries after the time of Jesus, but is thought to express a traditional concept extending perhaps to the first century or earlier. E.P. Sanders (*Jesus and Judaism*) has suggested this idea be called, "Covenantal Nomism," but Sanders errs by implying that this view was nearly universally held.

[115] The "Dead Sea Scroll" people sounded very much like Paul the Apostle; in *Justification and Variegated Nomism Volume I*, (D. A. Carson, editor, p. 394), contributor Markus Bockmuehl writes, "The Qumran psalmist acknowledges that his righteousness is the gift of God's righteousness, pre-ordained from all eternity." For a good summation of Essene belief regarding justification, see Bockmuel's chapter, pp.381-414.

An outsider might view the 613 *mitzvot* of the *First Testament* as oppressive restrictions, some sensible, some not. Godly Jews had a different viewpoint, viewing them as opportunities to do God's will. The Jews considered themselves advantaged because they possessed the Torah. Devout Israelites gloried in studying and fulfilling *mitzvot*.[116] The Jewish people still celebrate a festival called, "*Simchat Torah*" to celebrate the "Joy of the Torah." The festival is celebrated one or two days after *Sukkot*, the Feast of Tabernacles.[117]

When God regenerates an individual, that person develops a new love for God's Word. Notice that the Messianic Jewish believers in Acts 21:20[118] were often more "zealous for the Law" *after* believing in Yeshua than before. Their trust, however, was not in works righteousness through the Law, but rather the righteousness that God gives to those who

---

[116] As Spangler and Tverberg point out in *Sitting At the Feet of Rabbi Jesus* (pp.146-148), to many devout Jews, the Law provided them "opportunities to do good." The Torah was and is viewed positively, not merely as restrictive. Paul, in Romans 9:3-5, suggests that God gift of the Law to the Hebrews was a blessing and an advantage: "For I could wish that I myself were accursed, separated from Christ for the sake of my brethren, my kinsmen according to the flesh, who are Israelites, to whom belongs the adoption as sons, and the glory and the covenants and the giving of the Law and the temple service and the promises, whose are the fathers, and from whom is the Christ according to the flesh, who is over all, God blessed forever. Amen." The fact that "the promises" and "the Christ" are included in this list suggests that the entire list is made up of positive advantages (see also Romans 3:1-3). Commenting on Paul, Dr. Ron Moseley writes: "…Paul never attempted to start a new religion that opposed the Holy Scriptures. His arguments that appear to be directed against the Law were actually against the misuse of the Law…" (*Yeshua: A Guide to the Real Jesus and the Early Church*, p. 39).

[117] See *Building Bridges* by David A. Rausch, p.46.

[118] Acts 21:20 reads, "When they heard this, they praised God. Then they said to Paul: "You see, brother, how many thousands of Jews have believed, and **all of them are zealous for the law**."

trust Jesus.[119] Unfortunately, many other Jews who were zealous for the Law sought to be justified by it, rejecting Jesus or negating the need for his sacrifice.[120] One significant purposes of the Law is to lead those under the Law to Messiah Yeshua. *The Second Testament* itself clearly teaches that *some* Jews misused the Law, seeking to be justified by its observance.[121]

> ➤ *The Torah and the Kingdom of Heaven (God)*

Torah study was a privilege because when one studied, he "entered the Kingdom of Heaven," "took the yoke of the Kingdom of Heaven," or came "under the wing of heaven."[122] Note the words of Hillel and the Talmudic commentary that follow those words:

---

[119] In Galatians 2:15-16, the Apostle Paul writes: "We who are Jews by birth and not 'Gentile sinners' know that *a man is not justified by observing the law, but by faith in Jesus Christ.* So we, too, have put our faith in Christ Jesus that we may be justified by faith in Christ and not by observing the law, because by observing the law no one will be justified."

[120] In Galatians 2:21, Paul argues against those who claim to believe in Jesus but yet are seeking to be justified by Torah observance. Paul's argument is that if one could be saved by Torah observance, then Christ's death was unnecessary.

[121] Romans 10:2-4 makes the point. The "end" (goal) of the Law in this context is being justified by faith in Jesus Christ. Some who adhere to the "New Perspective" on Paul claim that Jews did not believe in works salvation. That claim is only partly true. As argued previously, first century Judaism was not the neat, cohesive package some present. See Luke 18:9 above.

[122] Even reciting the "Shema" was to enter the kingdom. Shmuel Safrai writes, "There is a story in rabbinic literature that helps illustrate the first-century Jewish understanding of the Kingdom of Heaven...A bridegroom is exempt from reciting the Shema on the first night of his marriage. . . . When Rabban Gamaliel married, he recited the Shema on the first night. His disciples said to him: 'Master, didn't you teach us that a bridegroom is exempt from reciting the Shema on the first night?' 'I will not listen to you,' he replied, 'so as to cast off from myself the Kingdom of Heaven even for a moment.' (*Mishnah, Berachot 2:5*)." Safrai's "sidebar" contribution to the article by Robert Lindsey, titled, " The Kingdom Of God: God's Power Among Believers" is from *The Jerusalem Perspective*, published January 1, 2004, www.jerusalemperspective.com, accessed 12-10-09.

> He [Hillel] would stand at the gate of Jerusalem and meet people going to work. He questioned them, "How much will you make at work today?" One person would answer, "A denarius." Another replied, "Two denarii." Then he would ask them, "What will you do with your earnings?" They would reply, "We will buy what we need to live." Then he challenged them, "Why don't you come follow me and acquire knowledge of the Torah. Then you will receive life in this world as well as life in the future world?" In this way Hillel lived all his days and was able to bring many people under the wing of heaven.[123]

Dr. David Flusser comments regarding the sages of *Bet Hillel*:

> In their opinion, what mattered was not whether one accepted Roman rule or rejected it; for the Kingdom of Heaven could come about at any time, once the people repented and took upon themselves the yoke of the Kingdom of Heaven – and once that happened, no nation or tongue would hold sway over them. Only then would God fulfill his promise to rule over Israel…the kingdom of Rome would vanish once the people had taken upon themselves the yoke of the Kingdom of Heaven…The Sages believed that even when a man recites "Hear O Israel," he is taking upon himself the Kingdom of Heaven and is living under it…Jesus developed the idea of the Kingdom of Heaven in a personal manner…It is reasonable to assume that…Jesus thought that he was not only at the center of this process, but that he was himself the Messiah, who was bringing the Kingdom of Heaven upon Israel."[124]

Since the Jews did not pronounce God's Name (Yahweh) and minimized pronouncing his personal titles (Lord, God, etc.), they would sometimes substitute *Ha Shem* ("the Name") or "Heaven" for God. Thus Jesus probably actually said, "The Kingdom of *Heaven*" (and "heaven" is used in Matthew's Gospel, the Gospel honed for Jewish readers), but the term

---

This commandment is not found in the Written Torah, but it is part of the Oral Torah. One was permitted, as it were, to put aside the Kingdom temporarily. Gamaliel, however, refused to forget about the Kingdom even for a few moments.

[123] *Avot R. Nat.,* vers. B, ch. 26, cited by Brad Young in *Meet the Rabbis*, p. 192.
[124] David Flusser, *Jewish Sources in Early Christianity*, pp. 50-54 *passim*.

is probably dynamically translated by Mark, Luke, and John for gentiles as "The Kingdom of *God*."

Our Matthew Texts

Matthew 6 and Matthew 19 include *Midrashim* based upon Deuteronomy 8. Yeshua explains that the principles of Deuteronomy 8 are relevant to the individual disciple on a daily basis. Matthew 6:24-34 reads:

> "No one can serve two masters. Either he will hate the one and love the other, or he will be devoted to the one and despise the other. You cannot serve both God and Money.
>
> "Therefore I tell you, do not worry about your life, what you will eat or drink; or about your body, what you will wear. Is not life more important than food, and the body more important than clothes? Look at the birds of the air; they do not sow or reap or store away in barns, and yet your heavenly Father feeds them. Are you not much more valuable than they? Who of you by worrying can add a single hour to his life?
>
> "And why do you worry about clothes? See how the lilies of the field grow. They do not labor or spin. Yet I tell you that not even Solomon in all his splendor was dressed like one of these. If that is how God clothes the grass of the field, which is here today and tomorrow is thrown into the fire, will he not much more clothe you, O you of little faith? So do not worry, saying, 'What shall we eat?' or 'What shall we drink?' or 'What shall we wear?' For the pagans run after all these things, and your heavenly Father knows that you need them. But seek first his kingdom and his righteousness, and all these things will be given to you as well. Therefore do not worry about tomorrow, for tomorrow will worry about itself. Each day has enough trouble of its own."

According to the *Mishnah*,

> Rabbi Simeon Alexander asked, "Have you ever seen a wild animal or a bird practicing a profession? Yet they have their sustenance provided for without anxiety and were they not created to serve me? But I was created to serve my Maker. How

much more then, should I have my sustenance provided for without anxiety. But I have done wrong and so I have given up my right to sustenance without worry."[125]

Jesus' admonition to trust God for daily needs was not unique; most sages preached a similar message. Yeshua promises that God will provide for his disciples and his children. What would he provide?

➢ *Food*

Rather than worry, Jesus admonishes his disciples to release their anxieties. "Is not life more important than food?" is close in meaning to, "Man does not live by bread alone." Yeshua illustrates the principle: God feeds the birds of the air; if he is concerned about mere birds, is he not concerned about you who are so much more valuable to God? Remembering the experiences of the Hebrews in the wilderness, we recall that God did allow them to go hungry for a time before he fed them. They also experienced intense thirst before he gave them water. Nonetheless, when he directed them into the dessert, he also provided for them. In like manner, the Savior promises that God would provide for Yeshua's disciples.

The Jewish people in Jesus' day were expected to provide hospitality for traveling rabbis and their disciples.[126] Despite the fact that respected Jews propagated this hospitality

---

[125] *m. Kiddushin 4:14*, cited by Brad H. Young, *Meet the Rabbis*, p. 73.
[126] Spangler, Ann and Tverberg, Lois, *Sitting at the Feet of Rabbi Jesus*, p. 14.

ethic, disciples were not *always* well-received.[127] It took faith to roam the countryside, far from home.

In other times and cultures, societies have not embraced a hospitality ethic toward Jesus' disciples. Have faithful Christians died from starvation? Sadly, yes. Although we cannot predict God's response to a need, the issue is God's *ability* to provide – when he chooses to do so.

Although God responds to faith, he is not controlled by it; it is God who animates faith and makes it effective. While interpreting these promises for God's special care, we must distinguish between (1) the immediate contexts, relating the hardships taken by the Twelve to follow their Master. Such hardships were common to Jewish disciples following a traveling sage in first century Palestine; (2) the hardships of the modern Christian disciple (in the process of training via a church family); and (3) the hardships that result from living in a cursed world.[128] During famine, for example, Christians suffer with the rest of humanity; we have yet to hear reports of manna falling from the skies once again! Yet when we trust the Lord to provide, he cares for us in amazing ways.

➢ *Clothing*

---

[127] Mark 6:11 evidences the possibility for disciples to be rejected, "And if any place will not welcome you or listen to you, shake the dust off your feet when you leave, as a testimony against them."

[128] Romans 8:22-23 (ESV) makes it clear that believers suffer along with the unregenerate in this life: "For we know that the whole creation has been groaning together in the pains of childbirth until now. And not only the creation, but we ourselves, who have the firstfruits of the Spirit, groan inwardly as we wait eagerly for adoption as sons, the redemption of our bodies."

God clothed the Hebrews during their sojourn by preserving their original clothing. The implication for Jesus' disciples is that God would provide some sort of clothing for those who temporarily set aside their vocations to learn from him; they need not fear. If God provides "garments" for the lilies of the field – even though they do not spin fabric – how much more concerned is he for Yeshua's *talmidim (disciples)*?

> *Look Around*

Moses commanded his people to "look back" at what God had done. Yeshua encourages his disciples to "look around" at the birds and the flowers. They, too, serve as reminders of God's faithfulness. Following the typical *Midrash* pattern, Yeshua brings home the point with an illustration in Matthew 6:26:

> Look at the birds of the air; they do not sow or reap or store away in barns, and yet your heavenly Father feeds them. Are you not much more valuable than they?

> *Discipleship Meant A Hiatus from One's Vocation, Not Its Abandonment*

Let me remind the reader that Deuteronomy 8:18[129] offers an important point for interpreting Jesus' words. Yeshua is not teaching that we simply trust Yahweh's faithfulness and do nothing to provide for ourselves. Yeshua's disciples had vocations

---

[129] "But remember the LORD your God, for it is he who gives you the ability to produce wealth, and so confirms his covenant, which he swore to your forefathers, as it is today."

and sometimes years of experience in those vocations. Jesus' disciples followed him "part time" for two years and "full time" for a little more than a year.[130]

After a disciple traveled with a sage and memorized his teachings, he would usually return to his trade, as would the rabbi.[131] After returning to work, he would probably embrace the work ethic enumerated in the *Second Testament*: work hard, spend wisely, support one's self, and give to others in need.[132]

> ➢ *Put God First and Be Blessed*

In Deuteronomy, Moses emphasized that if the Hebrews obeyed God's commands, they would prosper in the Promised Land. Yeshua takes this same principle and summarizes it in superb *Midrashic* form: "But seek first the kingdom of God and his righteousness, and all these things will be added to you" (Matthew 6:33).

Christ distills the relationship between God and his blessings as a matter of priority. If his disciples would seek Yahweh first, they could anticipate Yahweh's blessing. In this same context, Christ reminds us that sometimes those blessings come in the next life, and that our focus should be "the life to come." This is a spiritual application of the Deuteronomy text; Jesus is extending the principle.

Context is king, and nearby Matthew 6:19-21 (ESV) reads,

---

[130] Class notes from *The Synoptic Gospels* taught by Dr. Paul Benware, taught at Moody Bible Institute, Spring, 1978, commenting on Broadus' *Harmony of the Gospels*, paragraph 41.
[131] Bivin, David, *New Light on the Difficult Words of Jesus*, pp. 10-12.
[132] See I Thessalonians 4:11 and Ephesians 4:28.

> Do not lay up for yourselves treasures on earth, where moth and rust destroy and where thieves break in and steal, but lay up for yourselves treasures in heaven, where neither moth nor rust destroys and where thieves do not break in and steal. For where your treasure is, there your heart will be also.

> ➢ *The Temptation: Displacing God with Money*

We have three main resources: time, money, and energy. When we absorb an inordinate amount of time making money and thus expend all our energy, we must stop and re-examine our priorities. When our time and energy become depleted, our relationship to God and family usually suffer. Putting God first helps us organize the rest of life and connect the dots.

Seeking the Kingdom, and then enjoying "these things" presents the picture of a properly ordered life. Yeshua nowhere denies the teachings of Ecclesiastes, which urge us to enjoy life's simple pleasures.[133] But we must remember: "You cannot serve both God and Money."[134]

Camel Through the Eye of A Needle

---

[133] Ecclesiastes 5:18-20 is one of several passages that make the point: "Here is what I have seen to be good and fitting: to eat, to drink and enjoy oneself in all one's labor in which he toils under the sun during the few years of his life which God has given him; for this is his reward. Furthermore, as for every man to whom God has given riches and wealth, He has also empowered him to eat from them and to receive his reward and rejoice in his labor; this is the gift of God. For he will not often consider the years of his life, because God keeps him occupied with the gladness of his heart."

[134] Matthew 6:24b. It is in this sense that the pursuit of wealth can become an idol: Colossians 3:5 reads, "Put to death, therefore, whatever belongs to your earthly nature: sexual immorality, impurity, lust, evil desires and greed, which is idolatry." Unfortunately, the "idolatry" principle does not negate the vehement prohibition against literal idolatry, a problem that has troubled Christendom since Medieval times and is no longer taken seriously.

The Matthew 19:16-30 passage appears to be another *Midrash* based on the same Deuteronomy text. In this instance, the refusal of the rich young ruler to put Torah study above his wealth is the backdrop for Yeshua's hilarious illustration of a camel passing through the eye of a needle. The portion of this text that I will address is Matthew 19:22-26:

> But when the young man heard this statement, he went away grieving; for he was one who owned much property. And Jesus said to His disciples, "Truly I say to you, it is hard for a rich man to enter the kingdom of heaven.
>
> "Again I say to you, it is easier for a camel to go through the eye of a needle, than for a rich man to enter the kingdom of God."
>
> When the disciples heard this, they were very astonished and said, "Then who can be saved?"
>
> And looking at them Jesus said to them, "With people this is impossible, but with God all things are possible."

> ➢ *Yeshua and Humor*

The limited evidence we have implies that Jesus frequently used humor in his teaching. The Jewish culture has not only produced the world's greatest comedians, but some Rabbis viewed comedy as a spiritual ministry.[135]

A camel stringing through the eye of a needle is *intended* to be an absurd, sidesplitting picture. The expression does not signify an opening between rocks through which a camel can only pass with great difficulty. Some deprive Yeshua of his lighter side by

---

[135] Rabbi Simon Jacobson comments, "…the Zohar says something even stronger, that without humor, there is no wisdom. Without a sense of humor, one cannot really have wisdom. In other words, to open up a mind, a heart, to truly be able to understand things, humor plays a very significant role…" www.meaningfullife.com.

proposing the Syriac translation, which uses the word "rope" instead of camel.[136] Yeshua embraces the comedy of the absurd on more than one occasion. His jest about a man with a plank in his eye criticizing a man with a speck of sawdust in his eye is even more absurd.[137]

> ➤ *So What Is Jesus Saying Here?*

Is the Great Teacher advocating socialism, or giving all our savings to the poor? Jesus' respect for the *Tanakh* is beyond question. Throughout the *First Testament*, we note a correlation sometimes exists between wealth and godliness. Yeshua would not and could not deny this.

Abraham, called "the friend of God"[138] is the proto-type for "all who have faith."[139] Abraham was so wealthy in livestock that his prosperity created strife between he and his nephew, Lot.[140] He had servants, flocks, and herds. Isaac and Jacob inherited and multiplied this wealth. Job,[141] perhaps the godliest man of his day, was also among the wealthiest. Besides being the "man after God's own heart," King David was a leading monarch of his day – and amazingly wealthy.

---

[136] Matthew 9:24 reads, "Again I say to you, It is easier for a rope to go through the eye of a needle, than for a rich man to enter into the kingdom of God," George M. Lamsa, *The Holy Bible from Ancient Easter Manuscripts*, pp. 973-974.
[137] Luke 6:42
[138] James 2:23
[139] Romans 4:11,16
[140] Genesis 13:2 (KJV) reads, "And Abram was very rich in cattle, in silver, and in gold." Genesis 13:5ff describe the strife between him and Lot.
[141] See Job 1:3.

Nor is Jesus teaching gentile or secular *governments* how to run their economies. Yeshua's teachings are intended for *his disciples*, and they require *voluntary compliance* from those who embrace Him as Messiah. Good deeds are not an end in themselves; they should, when possible, be done "in my (i.e., *Jesus'*) name."[142]

Yeshua's *talmidim* (disciples) were *surprised* at his teaching. They assumed God's material blessing would follow obedience to his commands, as implied in the Deuteronomy passage. But the Deuteronomy passage begins with the Hebrews in a state of initial poverty. They then seek God, and later are made wealthy. Like the rich young ruler, many who attained wealth *first* would not typically take the time to follow a rabbi and study the Torah *later*, thus failing to come under the "yoke of the Kingdom." In this case, the rich young ruler claimed to have a heart for God. Yet, when he was put to the test, he did not embrace seeking the Kingdom of God above all else.[143]

This passage might be a "double *Midrash*," drawing not only from Deuteronomy, but also from I Kings 19:19-21.[144] Spangler and Tverberg point out that the rabbis viewed the

---

[142] Mark 9:41; the believer is to do good works simply out of compassion, but is also concerned that God be glorified in the process, when possible; see Matthew 5:16.

[143] See chapter ten.

[144] This passage offers the example of Elisha "selling all he has and giving it to the poor [people]. It reads, "So Elijah went from there and found Elisha son of Shaphat. He was plowing with twelve yoke of oxen, and he himself was driving the twelfth pair. Elijah went up to him and threw his cloak around him. Elisha then left his oxen and ran after Elijah. 'Let me kiss my father and mother good-by,' he said, 'and then I will come with you.'
'Go back,' Elijah replied. 'What have I done to you?'
 So Elisha left him and went back. He took his yoke of oxen and slaughtered them. He burned the plowing equipment to cook the meat and gave it to the people, and they ate. Then he set out to follow Elijah and became his attendant."

relationship of Elijah to Elisha as the perfect model for the rabbi-disciple relationship.[145]

We will contemplate Jesus' *Midrash* on discipleship in chapter ten, but it is very likely that Yeshua was not asking the rich man to dispose of all his wealth, but rather his lands and whatever would keep him from taking a hiatus to follow Yeshua.

In the ancient "Ethics of the Fathers" chapter 4, Rabbi Meier captures a similar concept:

> Lessen your work for worldly goods, and be busy in the Torah. Be humble of spirit before all people. If you neglect Torah, many causes for neglecting it will present themselves to you, but if you work in the Torah, He has abundant reward to give you.[146]

According to Yeshua, even someone like this rich young ruler was not without hope; with God, the camel *can* go through the eye of the needle: "nothing is impossible with God." Statistically, those absorbed with materialism and wealth are less likely to seek the Kingdom of God.[147] Yet God is able to work within the hardest heart.

Conclusion: Yahweh the Focus

The overall lesson of these *Midrashim* is clear: Rather than first seeking "success" and then adding a relationship to God as an afterthought, Yahweh demands his disciples make pursuing God the central priority of their lives.

---

[145] *Sitting at the Feet of Rabbi Jesus*, pp. 54-55.
[146] Quoted in *Meet the Rabbis* by Brad Young, p. 133.
[147] For another viewpoint on this story with some interesting insights, see David Bivin, *New Light on the Difficult Words of Jesus*, pp. 81-87.

Chapter 5: Midrashim on the Mount, Part Three: Lending and Perfection

(Deut. 15:7-11; Matt. 5:42; Deut. 18:13; Matt. 5:48)

In the trenches of life, we rely upon short principles that offer us immediate direction and hone our spiritual instincts. Some of these principles might include pithy sayings, such as "More is not always better."

For one who follows Jesus, the source for meaningful truisms is often the *Sermon on the Mount*. Most of us are fluent with the golden rule, "Do unto others as you would have them do unto you." Expressions like "turn the other cheek," or "walk the extra mile" have been incorporated into western culture because even the non-devout find them remarkably useful. The fact that many who reject the divinity of Christ and the basic tenants of Christianity value Yeshua's teaching suggest that he was no typical rabbi, nor were his *Midrashim* purely standard stock. His expertise and insight set him apart from the pack.[148] Of course, once we understand him to be the Messiah and true deity, our estimation soars way beyond that of a gifted teacher.

In this chapter, we will probe two texts from the *SOM* and trace their origin back to Deuteronomy. Both are succinct truisms, yet both are frequently misunderstood. In addition to being misunderstood, the agenda-driven can intentionally misuse them.

Lending and Repayment of Loans

---

[148] A number of passages suggest this, including Matthew 13:53-58 and Matthew 7:29.

Moses and Jesus address lending money to poor friends and acquaintances in Deut. 15:7-11 and Matt. 5:42. The Deuteronomy text reads:

> "If there is among you a poor man of your brethren, within any of the gates in your land which the LORD your God is giving you, you shall not harden your heart nor shut your hand from your poor brother, but you shall open your hand wide to him and willingly lend him sufficient for his need, whatever he needs. Beware lest there be a wicked thought in your heart, saying, 'The seventh year, the year of release, is at hand,' and your eye be evil against your poor brother and you give him nothing, and he cry out to the LORD against you, and it become sin among you. You shall surely give to him, and your heart should not be grieved when you give to him, because for this thing the LORD your God will bless you in all your works and in all to which you put your hand. For the poor will never cease from the land; therefore I command you, saying, 'You shall open your hand wide to your brother, to your poor and your needy, in your land'" (New King James Version).

I propose that Matthew 5:42 is a succinct summary of the Deuteronomy text cited above.

The Matthew passage reads:

> "Give to him who asks you, and from him who wants to borrow from you do not turn away."

> *Observations*

Returning to the mother text in Deuteronomy helps us to narrow the subject matter under examination. In Deuteronomy, the discussion is not about *indiscriminate* giving, but *knowledgeable* giving.

The text calls our attention to the poor within the community, people who are known to the potential donor. These are the unfortunate of the land. Although we might include beggars and an entire class of people referred to as "the poor," the discussion in Deuteronomy soon shifts toward making business loans, not merely giving alms.

> ➢ *Loans and the Sabbath Year*

Normally when one makes a loan, he anticipates being paid back. But the *mitzvah* regarding the Sabbath Year could make loaners hesitant to lend. This seventh year meant a cancellation of debt; if it was near at hand, the lender could lose all he loaned.[149] The case scenario is that of an unfortunate man who would normally receive a loan from a friendly neighbor; perhaps his crops failed while the friend reaped a bountiful harvest. In most years, neighbors might lend freely to one another to cover such eventualities or other unforeseen issues. But, because the Sabbath year loomed near, the friend refuses to make the loan. Thus the Sabbath year could become a detriment rather than a blessing. In Yeshua's statement documented in Matthew 5:42, the term "ask" and "borrow" are used in parallel, suggesting that the request is not that of a panhandler who wants cash for "a cup of coffee." We can infer that the one requesting help is known to us.[150] He is asking for a loan and intends to pay it back.[151] The loaner is not enabling the borrower to live irresponsibly or maintain an addiction.

---

[149] Deuteronomy 31:10 reads, "Then Moses commanded them: 'At the end of every seven years, in the year for canceling debts...'"
[150] The Torah includes a separate set of ethics for strangers, as demonstrated in Leviticus 19:10, for example.
[151] David Bivin and Roy Blizzard, Jr., point this out in *Understanding the Difficult Words of Jesus*, p. 74.

The reader must remember that Jesus is reducing detailed teaching down to general, "hands on" principles. He is demonstrating how Torah passages could be expanded and applied to life in his day. These condensed, black and white generalities provide a starting point, not necessarily an ending point. They are not complete treatises, but wise sayings which sometimes must be weighed against other wise sayings.[152]

We have no idea how many minutes of conversation are *not recorded* between Matthew 5:41 and 5:42 or 5:43, so we must assume that these are summaries of longer discussions. It is unlikely that Yeshua rattled off these truisms in machine-gun like rapidity.

> *Obeying Torah Requires Faith*

The Deuteronomy text demands that the loaner ignore the Sabbath "year of remission" consideration; instead of fearing loss, the loaner was to depend upon God to make good. Yahweh promises to bless the obedient lender and compensate him for his loss (in some appropriate way).

This does not imply that a loaner would lend indiscriminately in all cases, but it does mean that the loaner is forbidden to refrain from loaning money *because the Sabbath year was near.* He might choose to refrain from making a loan for other legitimate

---

[152] Matthew 7:6 (KJV) suggests that it can be wasteful to expend our efforts: "Give not that which is holy unto the dogs, neither cast ye your pearls before swine, lest they trample them under their feet, and turn again and rend you." Like Proverbs 26:4-5 (KJV), there are situations where one must discern an approach depending upon the character of the individual with whom we are interacting: "Answer not a fool according to his folly, lest thou also be like unto him. Answer a fool according to his folly, lest he be wise in his own conceit."

reasons, reasons not mentioned in the text (such as a track record of irresponsibility on the part of the borrower, for example).

All the Israelites were to embrace a compassionate attitude and an "open hand" toward a brother who was in a financial pinch because of misfortune. With the (in-theory) elimination of the irresponsible early in life,[153] extreme poverty would be connected to physical/mental handicap, misfortune (a widow with no children, for example), but not usually a poor work ethic. The fact that Solomon associates poverty with the sluggard suggests that laziness *was* an issue in some instances, and probably garnered no more sympathy in ancient Israel than that given by Paul in the first century: "For even when we were with you, we gave you this rule: 'If a man will not work, he shall not eat'" (2 Thessalonians 3:10). We can assume that the "worthy poor" are in mind.

> *Good Eye Bad Eye*

The Hebrew literally warns the potential loaner not to allow his "eye" to "become bad" toward his poor brother. This was a common idiom of the time: a "good eye" signifies a

---

[153] Deuteronomy 21:18-21 is worded to imply that irresponsibly behaving young teenagers were to be stoned, and that this would reinforce a responsible ethic in society, thus greatly reducing the number of "mooches" in the land. It reads, "If any man has a stubborn and rebellious son who will not obey his father or his mother, and when they chastise him, he will not even listen to them, then his father and mother shall seize him, and bring him out to the elders of his city at the gateway of his hometown.
"They shall say to the elders of his city, 'This son of ours is stubborn and rebellious, he will not obey us, **he is a glutton and a drunkard**.'
"Then all the men of his city shall stone him to death; so you shall remove the evil from your midst, and **all Israel will hear of it and fear**."

compassionate look resulting in generosity; and a "bad eye" refers to a harsh look without sympathy (producing no generosity).[154]

Jesus likewise used the idiom of the good or bad "eye" in Matthew 6:21-23 to refer to a generous (or stingy) disposition: "For where your treasure is, there your heart will be also. The eye is the lamp of the body. If your eyes are good, your whole body will be full of light. But if your eyes are bad, your whole body will be full of darkness. If then the light within you is darkness, how great is that darkness!"

Narrowing our discussion to loans and their relationship to the Sabbath year, I believe Yeshua is saying, "If you simply trust God and do what He says, God promises to bless you. If you honor the Sabbath year and the unsecured generosity it brings, God will provide." He is reasserting the clear instruction of the Deuteronomy passage.

On this issue, Yeshua seems to stand alone. Although the rabbis taught the importance of alms and compassion, they expended great effort to steer around the Sabbath year (release of all debts) *mitzvah*.[155]

> ➢ *Weaseling Out of Torah*

The *Talmud* reveals one rabbinic approach to circumvent the Sabbath year forgiveness of debt. If man A loans man B money and a Sabbath year approaches, man B is expected to

---

[154] See comments on Matthew 6:22-23 in *The Jewish New Testament Commentary* by David H. Stern, p. 32.
[155] Regarding the related observance of the Year of Jubilee, see *Jesus the Pharisee* by Harvey Falk, pp. 28-30. Falk offers evidence both for and against Jubilee being celebrated during Second Temple times.

pay back the loan – not as repayment, but as a "gift." We might compare the idea to a benefit with free admission but a mandatory "suggested donation." If the borrower refuses to call such repayment s a "present," the creditor can take extreme measures to force the debtor to mouth the words that his repayment is actually a gift:

> If a man repays another money which he owes him in the seventh year, the other should say to him, I remit it. If the debtor then says, 'All the same [take it]', he may take it from him. [This rule is based on] the text, Now this is the word of the release. Rabbah said: **The creditor may tie him up till he says so**. Abaye raised an objection [from the following]: When [the debtor] offers him the money he should not say, This is in payment of my debt, but, 'It is my [money] and **I make you a present of it**'? — Rabbah replied: yes; **he ties him up until he says so**.[156]

Hillel devised another loophole to avoid the loss associated with the Sabbath year. It is called the "prosbul." The system was simple: instead of loaning money to an individual, it was leant to the Jewish court, and the court lent it to the individual. Since the cancellation of debts applied only to fellow Hebrews (and not an institution), the debt cancellation could be avoided.[157]

Christ refutes these approaches and expects his disciples to follow the original intent and clear instruction of the Deuteronomy passage.

> ➢ *Application*

By way of application, Jesus teaches us that compassion needs to be a habit, not an event. Sometimes it means being patient and understanding; sometimes it means being

---

[156] *Gittin 37b*
[157] See "Prosbul" in the *Jewish Encyclopedia*, www.jewishencyclopedia.com, accessed 12-22-09.

generous; sometimes it means being friendly to someone who is alone and without friends; it always means concern. Compassion is not something you can always do in a controlled environment; it involves caring about people in neighborhoods and communities. Although soup kitchens, missions, and charities are important ways to make compassion proactive, the temptation to segregate and compartmentalize compassion as something done on behalf of strangers misses the point the Deuteronomy passage. Yeshua's disciples need to consider ministering to people at our places of employment, neighborhoods, and yes, within our church congregations. Hurting people are not simply "over there;" they are all around us, if we open our minds to see them.

Aiming for God's Standard (Deut. 18:13; Matt. 5:48)

Jesus addresses another topic, that of "perfection" or "blamelessness." In Matthew 5:48, Yeshua practically paraphrases Deuteronomy 18:13; note both passages:

"Be perfect, therefore, as your heavenly Father is perfect" (Matthew 5:48)

"You must be blameless before the LORD your God" (Deuteronomy 18:13).

The similarities when reading Deuteronomy 18:13 in the Septuagint are even more evident: "You shall be perfect before the Lord Your God."

Yeshua probably spoke and taught in Mishnaic Hebrew.[158] About two centuries before Jesus, a team of Jewish scholars translated the Hebrew Testament into Greek. This translation is called "The Septuagint" and is abbreviated "LXX" because 70 scholars purportedly did the translating. We often fail to remember that Yeshua's words were translated by the Gospel authors from Mishnaic Hebrew into Greek. This is why a comparison of Jesus' words in Matthew with the LXX of Deuteronomy is particularly relevant; both are translated from Hebrew into Greek.

The original word used in Deuteronomy is probably also the same word spoken by Yeshua, best translated into English as "blameless" rather than "perfect."

The Hebrew word for peace, *shalom*, is derived from the root word *shalem*, which means "wholeness and completion." It is bound up with the word *shlemut*, perfection – the goal towards which we can only aspire.[159] So to be "perfect" is to be at *complete peace with God and others*, at least as much as possible.[160] We are at peace with God when we are justified by faith in Jesus Christ[161] and when we subsequently walk closely with him.

---

[158] For an argument to this effect, see *Understanding the Difficult Words of Jesus* by David Bivin and Roy Blizzard Jr., pp. 1-65. Bivin also defines in the article "Online Glossary" from *Jerusalem Perspective* (http://www.jerusalemperspective.com/ default.aspx? tabid=53, accessed 1-19-10), "Mishnaic Hebrew — the Hebrew spoken in the land of Israel during the first centuries B.C./A.D., used loosely to refer to post-biblical Hebrew. Since this dialect is the language of the rabbinic works composed during the following centuries, it also is referred to as "rabbinic Hebrew." Some scholars prefer the term "Middle Hebrew."
[159] Keren Hannah Pryor, "*A Taste of Torah*" daily messianic devotional, "Emor 'Say,'" 10 May 2008
[160] This thought suggests added insight to Paul's words in Romans 12:18 (NASB), "If possible, so far as it depends on you, be at peace with all men."
[161] See Romans 5:1

Yeshua knows we are sinners and can never be blameless in the practical, absolute sense. Does he make this seemingly unrealistic demand merely to convict us of sin and remind us of our depravity before God? Although we cannot prove his intent, perhaps *part* of his intent was to reinforce the idea that "all have sinned and fall short of the glory of God."[162] But, on the other hand, people can and do earn the title "blameless" in the Biblical sense, and I think Yeshua's primary intent leads us in that direction. Individuals labeled "blameless" in Scripture are still obviously sinners.[163] Thus blameless is not the equivalent of "sinless." In some ways, the Biblical concept of blamelessness is exactly opposite of traditional Wesleyan "holiness" views.[164]

> ➢ *The Role Model Approach*

Yeshua takes the command to be blameless and attaches it directly to the character of God. God Himself is the standard of blamelessness his disciples should emulate. Rather than a mere code of 613 *mitzvot*, the very character of God is the rubric.

With the incarnation, Jesus demonstrated how Yahweh would live if confined to mortal limitations. Yeshua had no sin nature but was human like the pre-fallen Adam, and could

---

[162] Romans 3:23

[163] The following are described in Scripture as "blameless:" Noah (Genesis 6:9), David (2 Samuel 22:24), Job (Job 1:1), Zechariah and wife Elizabeth (Luke 1:6), and even common elders were to be chosen on the basis of being "blameless" (Titus 1:6).

[164] Holiness theology generally teaches that sanctified people are not exactly blameless because they make innocent mistakes, but that the sanctified are free from sin. The Biblical perspective, in this author's opinion, is that mortals are always sinners, but sinners (who still sin) can be described as blameless.

be tempted.[165] Thus his character becomes worthy of imitation; we do not imitate Jesus' life, for we have neither his authority nor unique mission. We have no authority to turn over tables, nor are we to roam the countryside with bands of disciples. Yet we are called upon to imitate his godly way of living, his truly perfect and blameless walk.[166] Thus Jesus' character helps us to understand how to "be perfect as your father in heaven is perfect."

If Yeshua is indeed restating and amplifying the *mitzvah* from Deuteronomy (to pursue blamelessness), we must remember that the sinner saved by grace can only be perfect in the sense of legal (forensic) righteousness. God chooses *to view us* as sinless because we are engulfed in the righteousness of the Savior. At conversion, we legally exchange our sinfulness for the righteousness of Jesus.[167] Yet if the Messiah is talking about the earthy walk (as I believe he is), Yeshua is not saying that we can be as perfect as the Father; he is, instead, setting a goal for us to strive *toward*.

> *Helpless Before God in Sin*

Those who are labeled as "blameless" in Scripture are usually blameless in their attention toward obeying the Torah and honoring God in their lives. The actual condition of our souls is another matter. Romans 3:23 explains the believer's past: "…for all have sinned

---

[165] Hebrews 4:14-15; yet he did not have the predisposition to sin that came with the Fall.
[166] I John 2:6 reads, "…whoever says he abides in him ought to walk in the same way in which he walked" (ESV);
[167] See 2 Corinthians 5:21, Galatians 2:16, and Romans 5:1-11; Zechariah 3:1-10 might be the source text from which Paul drew his various *Midrashim* regarding justification.

and fall short of the glory of God." The believer's present is described by I John 1:8 (NASB), "If we say that we have no sin, we are deceiving ourselves and the truth is not in us." The believer's future is perfect Christ-likeness: "But we know that when he appears, we shall be like him, for we shall see him as he is" (I John 3:2). For we who are born sinners, complete holiness is a future condition, not an earthly one.

We see this contrast between blamelessness marred by the reality of sin in the lives of devout believers, including Zechariah, the father of John the Baptist. Of Zechariah and his wife Elizabeth, Luke pens, "They were both righteous in the sight of God, walking blamelessly in all the commandments and requirements of the Lord" (Luke 1:6). Yet this same Zechariah refused to believe the angelic messenger! To believe that his wife Elizabeth and he would parent a child in their old age was not without precedent, so it was not that hard of a thing to believe (especially at the hand of angel!). The text further implies that the angel became angry at Zechariah's unbelief and disciplined him by making him mute until John was born.[168] Thus "blameless" people still sin, even to this extent.

Included in the idea "blamelessness" is the concept of amending sinful failures. Part of "blamelessness" is properly handling sin when we fail.

> *Amending Our Sins*

---

[168] Luke 1:5-23

Through saving faith in Jesus Christ, we have legal righteousness and peace with God – now. Yet in our relationships toward God and others, we are not always at peace; sometimes those tensions are caused by our sins. Thus we have the provision of confessing our sins to God and seeking reconciliation with those we have wronged.[169] Legally, the Christian may look like a new pristine blanket in God's eyes. From the human perspective, the truly godly believer resembles a quilt repaired by many patches. It is amazing what God can do with our lives, considering the pull of our sinful natures!

---

[169] I John 1:8-10, Matthew 5:24

Chapter 6: Midrashim on the Mount, Part Four: Midrashim Leviticus on the Mount

(Leviticus 19:17-18 with Matthew 5:21-24; Leviticus 19:15-16 with Matthew 7:1-5; Deuteronomy 19:15 with Mathew 18:15-17)

In an earlier era of history, small businesses would hold promotional contests by asking patrons to guess how many beans were in a jar. No one knows how many *Midrashim* Yeshua taught while expositing texts from the *First Testament*. After more than 1900 years, we are only beginning to discover some of them.

In chapter two, I suggested that Jesus favored Deuteronomy, but he did not limit his *Midrashim* to Deuteronomy; they are drawn from passages throughout the *First Testament*. In this chapter, we will examine some important texts from Leviticus, texts which I believe serve as the source for another significant portion of the *Sermon on the Mount*.

Once again we will examine several *SOM* passages in symphony with their mother passages. We will delve into two themes: *judging rightly* and *conflict management*.

Judging Rightly

The idea of judgment – in both English and the ancient languages – sometimes refers to the concept of making wise and righteous decisions. We speak of a sensible person as a person of good judgment. Judging can also take a negative bent, meaning a critical, fault-finding attitude. The difference between discernment and harsh criticism can be subjective, depending upon what side of an issue we find ourselves.

Here is the text from Leviticus 19:15-16,

> "You shall do no injustice in court. You shall not be partial to the poor or defer to the great, but in righteousness shall you judge your neighbor. You shall not go around as a slanderer among your people, and you shall not stand up against the life of your neighbor: I am the LORD." (ESV)

And the corresponding text from Matthew 7:1-5,

> "Judge not, that you be not judged. For with the judgment you pronounce you will be judged, and with the measure you use it will be measured to you. Why do you see the speck that is in your brother's eye, but do not notice the log that is in your own eye? Or how can you say to your brother, 'Let me take the speck out of your eye,' when there is the log in your own eye? You hypocrite, first take the log out of your own eye, and then you will see clearly to take the speck out of your brother's eye." (ESV)

> ➢ *Consistent Judgment: No Double Standards*

The ancient rabbis warned about both favoring the poor out of sympathy and the rich out of personal advantage.[170] Solomon says, "Acquitting the guilty and condemning the

---

[170] Yitzchak Etshalom, commenting on Exodus 23:6-7, presents the traditional Jewish viewpoint: "The judge, apprised of the demands of compassion placed upon him, might pervert justice due to that selfsame compassion.' The poor man is so much needier,' thinks the compassionate judge, 'the rich can afford to lose; the poor man is probably innocent; I must show him mercy.' The Torah warns of that perversion … 'Distance yourself from a false matter...do not take graft.' The false matter and the graft referred to here are internal: i.e. the rationalizations with which we blind ourselves (see BT Shavuot 30). We ignore the trespasses of friends much as we turn a blind eye to the righteousness of our enemies; neither fits the image we'd like to maintain. The judge must be wary of this potential in his own psyche. His compassion is the necessary starting point; judging without soul is judging without the image of God. The fairness which must overrule compassion is the crowning feature of the judge. A judge who is fair without feeling the tension of sympathy is not a man; the judge who allows his sympathy to decide the case is not a judge." [source: *www.torah.org*, accessed 1-29-10]

innocent— the LORD detests them both."[171] Some Christian *niceniks* imply that Jesus breaks from the Torah. They claim he advocates allowing transgressions against society go unpunished in the name of love; thus, when Christians seek justice, they are considered hypocrites *a priori*. When asked, "What would Jesus do?" the *niceniks* respond, "Release the offender in love."

But when we discuss being loving, we must ask, "Loving to whom?" How loving is such passivity to the offender's past or potentially future victims? Matters are not that simplistic.[172]

Yeshua's words neither diminish nor alter the Torah; instead, they make the Torah teaching *more* applicable for daily life. This extension of Torah – not its reduction – is the nature of *Midrash*.

Countless scholars and laymen insist upon discontinuity between the teachings of Christ and the Mosaic Torah.[173] Thus, they imagine the Messiah's command ("Judge not") as a shift and departure from Mosaic instruction. Such a viewpoint does not reflect actual

---

[171] Proverbs 17:15

[172] Some Christians come to the "nicenik" position based upon a few Scriptures that *seem* to advocate that position. I would argue that the larger context of Scripture demonstrates that the "nicenik" position is based upon naive interpretation. Where persecution is legal, for example, Christians have no legal redress and must bear persecution when they cannot avoid it. In the case of Christians who are enslaved, they suffer a similar fate because there is no legal way to prosecute. Thus I Peter 2:20-24 is written to slaves in that situation. Paul, on the other hand, took advantage of his rights as a Roman citizen, which included protection from persecution (Acts 25:13ff).

[173] If not understood as selected portions of *Midrashim*, the SOM and the Torah can and do appear contradictory. It is the very concept of the "*Midrash* key" that harmonizes them.

scriptural understanding or practice; we find pro-active judging expected and demanded. The issue is not whether we *should* judge others, but rather *how* we judge others.[174] Once we doubt the consistency of Scripture, we open the door for rationalizations and non-biblical alternatives. The agenda-driven accept what suits their purposes (or matches their party line) and reject what stands in the way. *This agenda-driven mentality is exactly what both Torah and Jesus target. Judging by a double, inconsistent, agenda-driven, and unfair standard is unethical.*

Biblical interpretation is itself a matter of judgment and must be approached fairly: one must either reject all Scripture or somehow integrate all Scripture if one desires to be fair and consistent. We must assert that nothing commanded by God can be *intrinsically* wrong, even if it is a concession. Certain texts may not be applicable to all situations or all people or all times,[175] but what God commands cannot be wrong – at least under certain conditions. In some instances, those conditions may be entirely past.[176]

> ➤ *Stricter than God*

---

[174] In John 7:24 (NASB), Yeshua says, "Do not judge according to appearance, but judge with righteous judgment." This Christ calls upon us to proactively judge, but in a *righteous* way.

[175] The difference between *description* (what happened in a given situation or direction from God about a specific situation) needs to be distinguished from *prescription* (what God commands to be the normal procedure, the perennial mode of operation). Even in the realm of prescription, we must also inquire as *to whom and for when* the prescription was written.

[176] A simple case in point is God destroying the entire world with a flood. He will not do so again, though he was not wrong to do so in the past (see Genesis 9:11). See the above note about the distinction between *description* and *prescription.* We might even add another category: a one-time (or limited time) *prescription* (as in the conquest of Canaan).

Jesus adds a clarifying point: the standards we use to judge others are the standards by which we will be judged; if we are stricter than God in our judgment of others, God will judge us by that same stricter standard.

People frequently chuckle when I make the claim that the Pharisees were stricter than God. Because many of us have embraced the wrong idea that God's standards are *always* stricter than man's, I would point to the example of Yeshua himself as a proof for this idea. He lived a sinless life, yet *he did not meet the standards of some Pharisees*. He was condemned because he did not fast frequently enough; he was accused of eating too much, drinking too much, hanging around the wrong crowds, and violating the Sabbath Day command.[177] Yet none of these "violations" were actual violations of the written Torah; they were violations of man-made religion and additions to the Torah, standards mostly championed by the *Bet Shammai*.[178] Within Judaism we can note many standards which are stricter than God's.[179]

---

[177] Matthew 11:18-19 reads, "For John came neither eating nor drinking, and they say, 'He has a demon.' The Son of Man came eating and drinking, and they say, 'Here is a glutton and a drunkard, a friend of tax collectors and "sinners." 'But wisdom is proved right by her actions." Matthew 12:1-13 offers an example of Yeshua being accused of violating the Sabbath because he refused to obey the man-made restrictions added to the Torah. As pointed out earlier, many of the Pharisees who denounced Jesus as not being stringent enough were almost certainly from the School of Shammai, not Hillel.

[178] See especially pp. 148-159 of *Jesus the Pharisee* by Harvey Falk. Falk is a major advocate of the view that most of Jesus' confrontations were with the School of Shammai.

[179] In a sense, Karaite Jews are a reaction to this dogmatic tedium. According to Wikipedia, Karaite Judaism is "… a Jewish movement characterized by the recognition of the *Tanakh* as is religious authority. Karaites maintain that all of the commandments handed down by Moses were recorded in the written Torah, and that an Oral Law was not given at Mount Sinai. As a result, Karaite Jews do not accept the Mishnah, *Talmud*, or Rabbinic decrees as binding. Karaite Judaism does not reject the *Talmud*, but holds

Controlling people are often motivated by fear, and fear might explain why Jewish leaders accumulated such tedious and trite rulings. The Talmud abounds with them. Realizing that the Talmud mostly documents the teachings of *Bet Hillel*, we hesitate to imagine the harsher and more tedious rules advocated by *Bet Shammai*. In some ways, Judaism resembles Catholicism in that both religions consider themselves bound by accumulated tradition and not by Scripture alone.

Some assume Yeshua's words, "Judge not lest you be judged" to imply that judging others can result in damnation. Thus, to the popular ear, salvation can be lost by being judgmental – or gained by refraining from judging others. The reader needs to note that this passage is speaking of *judgment*,[180] *not* necessarily damnation or salvation. Solomon assures us that "…God will bring every deed into judgment, including every hidden thing, whether it is good or evil" (Ecclesiastes 12:14). For the unregenerate, this judgment precedes being cast into the Lake of Fire; for the believer, this judgment occurs at the "judgment seat of Christ," and precedes entrance into heaven. In this case, judgment deals with *rewards in heaven and accountability*, not whether heaven or hell is

---

every interpretation of the *Tanakh* to the same scrutiny regardless of its source." [Source: http://en.wikipedia.org/wiki/Karaite_Judaism, accessed 2-8-10].

[180] D.A. Carson writes, " 'Do not be judgmental,' Jesus says, and then adds, 'or you too will be judged' (7:1). The latter clause may perhaps be taken like the first: if you are judgmental, others will be judgmental toward you. Alternatively, depending on the ambiguity of the Greek verb, the sentence may mean: do not be judgmental, or you will be condemned (whether by God or others). Either way, the clause adds stinging pungency to the injunction…" (D.A. Carson, *The Sermon on the Mount*, p. 100).

our destiny.[181] Although the destiny of humankind does fork in two directions (heaven or hell), neither heaven nor hell are socialistic (equal) in nature. Some are blessed in heaven more than others, while some are punished more in hell more than others.[182]

> *Fair Judgment*

Being fair means weighing matters from both perspectives and seeking to be unbiased and objective. From the perspective of a judge of any kind, it means exalting justice above personal agendas or relationships. In the daily life of a believer, we must cast our lot with what is right – over and above preferences, passions, or feelings. God's Word is our criteria, while the law of the land becomes our rubric if we are serving on jury duty, etc.[183]

> *Our Deceitful Hearts Throw a Wrench in the Machinery*

The Scriptures clearly state: "The heart is deceitful above all things and desperately wicked…." (Jeremiah 17:9a, KJV). Brain expert Dr. Richard Restak has documented how difficult it is for us to remain objective when we make decisions regarding ourselves

---

[181] See 2 Corinthians 5:10, Romans 14:10, Revelation 20:11-15. All of us are judged according to works; the lost are judged to determined *how severely* they will be punished in the lake of fire, the saved for *how honored* they will be in heaven. This is not to say that the believer should not stand in fear of God's judgment – some will "be saved but so as by fire" (I Corinthians 3:15).

[182] Mark 12:40, speaking of *some* hypocritical Pharisees, is one example of differing degrees of condemnation, "…who devour widows' houses, and for appearance's sake offer long prayers; these will receive *greater* condemnation."

[183] The problem of conflict between God's Word and men's rules presents a significant issue for study, but is well beyond the scope of this book.

or our immediate families. In *The New Brain*, Restak refers to research done by Dean Shibata of the University of Washington (Seattle):

> "Shibata finds that making decisions that affect you personally enhances activity in part of your frontal lobes…As a rule, you do not activate that area when thinking about events that do not involve your personally. 'When people make decisions that affect their own lives, they will utilize emotional parts of the brain, even though the task itself may not seem emotional,' says Shibata.
>
> "…But keeping our reasoning power uncontaminated by our emotions isn't as easily accomplished as we have been led to believe. Many times the influence of our emotions on our reasoning impedes self-knowledge…" [184]

Indeed, we do deceive ourselves. This is one reason for repeated Scriptural admonitions to seek counsel from *others*.[185] Those beyond immediate family are able to perceive our personal matters more objectively than we can. It takes great humility to consider one's own heart deceitful and desperately wicked! Many of us consider ourselves always objective and exempt from a deceitful heart; we do so at our own peril. This way of thinking itself is another evidence of our deceitful hearts.

> ➢ *Avoiding Destructive Attitudes*

In Leviticus, Yahweh warns his people not to slander. In the corresponding Mathew text, Yeshua constructs another fence to help us guard against slandering. This fence is our refusal to embrace a critical, cynical attitude. By embracing humility and taking the stance of being stricter about our own conduct than we are about the conduct of others,

---

[184] Restak, Richard, *The New Brain*, pp. 112-113.
[185] Proverbs 15:22 reads, "Plans fail for lack of counsel, but with many advisers they succeed."

we add a safety margin. We hold ourselves to the highest standard and hold others to a lesser standard.

As a good Rabbi who sought to be effective in *Midrash,* Jesus follows protocol and illustrates the point. Christ uses comical hyperbole, the exaggerated illustration of the log and the sliver (speck). Perhaps his disciples rolled in laughter as Yeshua told the story of a man walking around with a log (or beam) protruding from his eye. This is comedy of the most absurd kind. To make the story even more hilarious, the man with this log jutting from his eye has the nerve to criticize a man who has a tiny sliver or speck in his eye. What bold-faced hypocrisy! Interestingly, Jesus asserts the right (and obligation) of the man with the log to criticize his friend with the sliver – but only after he has first removed the log impeding his vision. While embracing the main point of the illustration, we must not forget this secondary point. Even a sliver needs to be addressed – by one who is positioned to do so.

But how does criticism and hypocrisy relate to the broader theme of slandering others? If we slander our brother, **we** now have a log in our eye. The legitimate concern we have with our brother is overshadowed by our greater sin. Our own credibility now becomes the focus. Being more stringent with ourselves – and confronting others properly – can keep us from losing our spiritual leverage with others.

> ➢ *Not About Judging Unbelievers*

As citizens and human beings, we are not wrong to make the world more civil,[186] but we should not confuse this with our main calling as God's saints. Our main goal is not to police *lost* people. Listen to Paul's words in I Corinthians 5:12-13a, "What business is it of mine to judge those outside the church? Are you not to judge those inside? God will judge those outside."

Although unbelieving people may perceive the believing community as judgmental because we do not engage in sinful behaviors,[187] they should not think us judgmental because we evidence a critical, negative spirit. One of our goals should be to encourage the *regenerate* to live in light of the Kingdom's standards while *seeking to reach the unregenerate* with the Gospel, not to coerce unregenerate people to act as though regenerate.[188]

Conflict Management

Another set of corresponding passages addresses the related subject of conflict management. Humble confrontation is an alternative to sinful judging and its cousin,

---

[186] We have already spoken extensively of the Noahide commands and the Covenant of Genesis 9:1-17. It seems believers do have a right to expect even lost society to abide by the covenant, since it was made with all mankind and since the rainbow still appears.

[187] The Bible teaches that even our quiet abstention from sinful practices can bring resentment. I particularly like the King James Version wording of I Peter 4:4, "Wherein they think it strange that ye run not with them to the same excess of riot, speaking evil of you."

[188] This does not mean we should not participate in the political process or take a stand on the moral issues of our day. But the focus of a congregation should be primarily spiritual growth. The believing citizen must carry his convictions into the voter's booth and has every bit as much a right to share his views as does any other citizen, but, unlike others, he must never abandon seeking to be fair, balanced, honest, and kind. Being fair is particularly out of vogue in our day, especially in political debate. Seeing the opposition as wholly evil and allies as wholly good evidences a lack of fair assessment.

slander. Confrontation can preclude slander and keep us from developing a judgmental attitude. Slander is the cowardly approach; confrontation requires courage.

> *Passages Involved*

Please note these four passages in two sets. Each Torah portion is coupled with a related (*Midrash*) portion from Matthew's Gospel.

Set one

Leviticus 19:17-18

> Do not hate your brother in your heart. Rebuke your neighbor frankly so you will not share in his guilt. Do not seek revenge or bear a grudge against one of your people, but love your neighbor as yourself. I am the LORD.

Matthew 5:21-24

> "You have heard that it was said to the people long ago, 'Do not murder, and anyone who murders will be subject to judgment.' But I tell you that anyone who is angry with his brother will be subject to judgment. Again, anyone who says to his brother, 'Raca,' is answerable to the Sanhedrin. But anyone who says, 'You fool!' will be in danger of the fire of hell.[189]

---

[189] Being in danger of the "fire of hell" for calling someone a fool seems particularly harsh and might seem to smack of works salvation (or at least loss of salvation). One issue in first century Judaism was how seriously one dealt with insult. John Gill points out that the *Zohar* (much later) records this ruling: "… it is forbidden a man to call his neighbor by a name of reproach everyone that calls his neighbor, 'a wicked man', shall be brought down to hell…" [Zohar in Exod. fol. 50.3]. Gill also cites a *Talmud* passage: "he that calls his neighbor a 'servant,' let him be excommunicated; a 'bastard,' let him be beaten with forty stripes; 'a wicked man', let him descend with him into his life or livelihood [Vid. T. Bab. Beracot, fol. 32. 2. Zohar in Exod. fol. 50. 2]; both cited by John Gill (quoted from http://www.studylight.org, Gill's commentary on Matthew 5:22, accessed 3-15-10, www.biblestudytools.com). Raca means a "numbskull" and "fool" means a wicked and foolish man. Still, why would Yeshua make such a big deal out of a relatively minor sin (who hasn't lost his temper and called someone a name sometime or other?). Some suggest that the word for "hell" really is the "Valley of Ben Hinnom," a location used by Jesus as a visual illustration of hell. Thus some suggest that Yeshua was talking about death by burning. Still, it seems much for the infraction stated. The answer to this question is still forthcoming!

"Therefore, if you are offering your gift at the altar and there remember that your brother has something against you, leave your gift there in front of the altar. First go and be reconciled to your brother; then come and offer your gift."

Set two

Deuteronomy 19:15

One witness is not enough to convict a man accused of any crime or offense he may have committed. A matter must be established by the testimony of two or three witnesses.

Matthew 18:15-17

"If your brother sins against you, go and show him his fault, just between the two of you. If he listens to you, you have won your brother over. But if he will not listen, take one or two others along, so that 'every matter may be established by the testimony of two or three witnesses.' If he refuses to listen to them, tell it to the church; and if he refuses to listen even to the church, treat him as you would a pagan or a tax collector."

> *Preventing Hatred Through Confrontation*

Apparently one area of debate within the Jewish community was the distinction between revenge and a grudge. The *Talmud* addresses this issue:

What is called revenge, and what is called bearing a grudge? Revenge is such a case: When one comes to the other, and asks him to lend a sickle to him, he says: Nay. On the morrow, the second comes to the first, and wants to borrow an axe. He answers: I do not wish to lend to you, as you have not lent to me. This is called revenge. What is bearing a grudge? When one comes to another, and asks him to loan him an axe, and does not get it. On the morrow the second comes to the first, and wants to borrow a shirt. He answers: I lend it to you, because I am not like you, who did not want to lend me yesterday. This is called bearing a grudge.[190]

---

[190] Tractate Yoma, Chapter 2 (aka, 23a).

Couched within this ruling is the idea that revenge is an action, whereas bearing a grudge is an attitude. One might bear a grudge and then take revenge, or one might bear a grudge and not take revenge – but still be bitter.

Yeshua demands that His disciples neither take revenge nor nurse a grudge. Jesus was not the only rabbi who took Leviticus 19 to heart. The *Talmud* again records:

> Did not Rabha say: He who leaves his injuries unavenged, will have his sins forgiven in Heaven? That means, if the offender comes to propitiate him, he should pardon.[191]

Like Yeshua, the sages understood our obligation to forgive those who have wronged us – assuming their repentance, in my understanding. What the Savior provides for us in Matthew 5 and 18 is a mechanism – a plan – to help us avoid taking revenge or holding a grudge. It is a plan to implement the Leviticus command, "Rebuke your neighbor frankly" (Leviticus 19:17a). This practical implementation of a Torah *mitzvot* is perhaps the central purpose of *Midrash.*

> ➢ *The Temptation toward Passivity and Denial*

Many of Yeshua's modern disciples believe that absorbing aggravations and quietly suffering abuse is the Christian approach to conflict. While suffering abuse may be part of our calling when it comes to religious persecution,[192] a passive role is not the Christian

---

[191] Tractate Yoma (Day of Atonement), Chapter 2.

[192] Matthew 5:10-12 (KJV) is discussing religious persecution in a summary fashion: "Blessed are they which are persecuted for righteousness' sake: for theirs is the kingdom of heaven. Blessed are ye, when men shall revile you, and persecute you, and shall say all manner of evil against you falsely, for my sake. Rejoice, and be exceeding glad: for great is your reward in heaven: for so persecuted they the prophets which were before you."

norm. This passive role – absorbing our aggravations – is the perfect climate for nurturing and culturing a grudge. Another temptation is to deny our feelings of anger, bitterness, or even hatred toward another. Denial is lying and is never the right approach. It is much better to be honest with ourselves, admit that we hate another, and do what we can to reconcile (if reconciliation is impossible). This is obviously not possible in every situation, particularly when we are dealing with unbelievers. Even in such instances, we are told to leave revenge to God (Romans 12:18-20). In some cases, the desire for revenge is not wrong,[193] but we must refuse to seek our own vengeance.

> *Confrontation and Covering Wrongs in Love*

What do we confront about, every infraction or irritation? I Peter 4:8 suggests that sometimes we need to let wrongs pass: "Above all, love each other deeply, because love covers over a multitude of sins." This passage is not about meriting forgiveness, but our obligation to love other believers. One way to demonstrate love is to overlook those minor sins and infractions. This passage is likely a paraphrase and perhaps *Midrash* of Proverbs 10:12b, "Hatred stirs up dissension, but love covers over all wrongs." Allowing

---

[193] The desire for revenge can be a function of the image of God in us; since God is a just God, we too sense a draw to demand it. Even the holy souls of martyrs under the altar in heaven desire revenge, so the desire for revenge can be holy. Revelation 6:9-11 reads, "When he opened the fifth seal, I saw under the altar the souls of those who had been slain because of the word of God and the testimony they had maintained. They called out in a loud voice, *'How long, Sovereign Lord, holy and true, until you judge the inhabitants of the earth and avenge our blood?'* Then each of them was given a white robe, and they were told to wait a little longer, until the number of their fellow servants and brothers who were to be killed as they had been was completed." Rather than receive a scolding, their desire for revenge is validated.

for the human element – including failings and sins – is part of building strong relationships.

When a believer clearly goes over the line[194] – or is doing something that negatively affects our attitude or relationship to that individual (even if it is not over the line) – then we should attempt to confront that person. If we fail to confront and resolve such issues, it is human nature to distance ourselves from that individual, and we are tempted to slander that person in one way or another.[195] This is not God's method for handling conflict – at least, not as a first step.

Although Peter – not Yeshua – adds this point, we need to remember that Yeshua's teachings are only partly recorded, and he is painting with a broad brush. Neither he nor Peter addresses all eventualities.

> ➤ *The Risk of Offering Criticism*

Proverbs 15:32 reads, "He who ignores discipline despises himself, but whoever heeds correction gains understanding." Paul contributes to this *Midrash* theme: "Brothers, if

---

[194] In I Corinthians 5:11 (NASB), Paul lists the type of sins that require excommunication if the offender refuses to repent; these are sins we should certainly confront a fellow believer about: "But actually, I wrote to you not to associate with any so-called brother if he is an immoral person, or covetous, or an idolater, or a reviler, or a drunkard, or a swindler–not even to eat with such a one." Whereas idolatry (bowing before an image) is a clear sin, it can be difficult to determine where we draw the line in matters of covetousness. Apparently, however, a line exists or these verses would be meaningless.

[195] The "deceitful heart" problem means that many of us believe we can avoid confrontation without hating or distancing ourselves from others; we are, in essence, claiming to be more spiritual than those who actually obey and confront!

someone is caught in a sin, you who are spiritual should restore him *gently*" (Galatians 6:1a).

Some persons do not respond reasonably to criticism, even if the confronter exemplifies humility and genuine concern. The offender may become defensive and play the "don't judge me" card. The non-repentant offender can perceive truly Biblical confrontation as judgmental.

Ironically, the person who accuses the confronter of "judging" is, in essence, himself judging (and condemning) the confronter! We have here a classic case of the double standard.[196]

> ➢ *A Reasonable Process*

Matters of debate between rabbis included how to implement the *mitzvot*. Contrast later Rabbinic opinion:

> How far should you go in admonishing people? Rav said: Until they beat you up for reprimanding them (Arachin 16b)…I might think that you should admonish him even if his face turned white for shame for being humiliated publicly…[197]

---

[196] The Bible encourages us to judge (but to judge rightly) in a number of passages. They include Luke 12:57, and Acts 14:9. I Corinthians 2:15 reads, "The spiritual man makes judgments about all things…" Jesus himself said: "Stop judging by mere appearances, and make a right judgment…" John 7:24. The word meaning judgment can refer to being discerning, decisive, or predisposed to be critical. The last definition is the problematic sort of judging condemned in Scripture.

[197] Cited by Avraham Yaakov Finkel in *The Torah Revealed*, p. 182.

Yeshua suggests a more reasonable format as the norm for handling conflict.[198] He establishes another fence, a procedure that can help you avoid becoming bitter or nursing hatred within your heart.

When *we* have wronged someone, we prioritize reconciliation over and above even religious obligations. The Jewish believer is urged to leave his sacrificial animal at the altar; he is to first be reconciled before making the offering.[199] Jesus spells out the process.

1. Begin at the Private Level

We are to speak to the individual, ideally face-to-face. Wisdom dictates we should be considerate of time and place. If the offender responds positively, the matter is closed.

2. Bring Others

If the offender refuses to repent, Yeshua instructs us to take along one or two others. This is a *Midrash* from the Deuteronomy 19:15 text, applied more broadly as is typical with *Midrash*. If the offender responds, the matter is closed.

3. Break Fellowship

If these approaches prove fruitless, then the church (probably a reference to its elders) must pass judgment on the situation. In that case, the unrepentant offender is shunned from fellowship until he becomes repentant.

---

[198] Matthew 18:15-17, cited in the text above.
[199] A Christian equivalent might be, "I will make an attempt to reconcile before I partake of communion."

This process is practical for at least three reasons. The first is that it assures that every effort was made to reclaim the sinner. The second reason is defensive, to protect the conscience of the offended party. The third is to reinforce an atmosphere of fair, orderly, objective judgment – even in the midst of conflict.[200]

Summary

Yeshua's disciples understand that absorbing or stuffing the wrongs done to us resuls in grudges and bitterness. Confrontation may be more uncomfortable for some than others, but the Master Teacher nowhere excuses us from following his teachings. If we confront a brother or sister for no other reason than honoring God, we are confronting for the best possible reason.

---

[200] The fence Yeshua constructed and the procedure he advocates helps his disciples implement the Levitical command and should be the norm for the above-stated reasons. How we implement these principles – particularly excommunication – may vary with the situation. Sometimes, for example, an individual can be removed from church membership (and fellowship) tactfully, out of concern for minor children, etc., who might be affected. Yeshua's words do not demand we broadcast a matter to all members; communication can be discreet. As in many matters, we must be more concerned about the victims who suffer than we are about the perpetrators. I cannot state this enough: many of the Messiah's *SOM* teachings address the typical or the norm, not every possible situation.

Chapter 7: Love for God and Others

(Deuteronomy 7:6-11 with John 3:16, 5:20-24, 14:21; Deuteronomy 10:18-19, Leviticus 19:18 with Luke 6:31, 10:25-37)

Chinese cooks are famous for combining sweet and sour flavors. Some people like sweet but not sour, while others prefer the sour and dislike the sweet. For many of us, however, sweet and sour harmonize into a perfect contrast.

We might consider God to have "sweet and sour" attributes. Although secular society and many Christians reject the idea of a God who is raging with wrath, the picture of a loving, forgiving God is quite popular. On one hand, we should not hesitate to declare the truth that God is a God of wrath (sour), despite its unpopularity. On the other hand, we should not overreact and downplay the wonders of his love (sweet). The believer is among those who have fled his wrath and escaped to his love.

The love of God – and our responsibility to love him and others – is clearly a major theme in Scripture. Perhaps the Bible emphasizes God's quality of holiness most,[201] but his love and grace follow closely behind.

Authors write volume after volume about the meaning and implications of love. Some approach love from a philosophical perspective, others deal with Biblical usage and

---

[201] Consider, for example, that the only Person of the Trinity Who is named after an attribute of God is the HOLY Spirit. It is noteworthy that the Holy Spirit is the agency of God's outpoured love into our hearts (Romans 5:5), and his first-listed "fruit" in our lives is love; he is usually called the *Holy* Spirit and *never* the Loving Spirit.

examine the original languages. We will casually touch on a few aspects of love that heighten our understanding via *Midrash*.

For purposes of discussion, my working definition of love is **"considering and acting upon what is in the beloved's best interest**." Love includes looking out for others.[202] Yet love is not necessarily about *pleasing* others. The exception is *marital* love, a love that includes intentional effort to please one's spouse.[203]

By Rabbinic calculation, the Torah contains 613 *mitzvot*. No particular Jew has ever been in a position to obey them all. Some of the 613 are gender-specific;[204] others pertain only to priests, etc. The spiritual, moral and relational commands – applicable to the average person – are summarized broadly within the 10 Commandments. The sages, including Rabbi Jesus, distilled them even more concisely.

Yeshua advocated that the *Two Great Commandments* were the ideal summary of the Torah. We may compare them to the forest overview, while the many trees represent the

---

[202] Philippians 2:4 is to the point: "Each of you should look not only to your own interests, but also to the interests of others."
[203] See I Corinthians 7:32-34
[204] Because many of us may not understand the passion devout Jews had for obeying *mitzvot* (commands and precepts), non-Jews often assign wrong motives to rabbinic statements. For example, devout Jews would bless God that they were not "born women." This fact has been misused to imply that the men looked down upon women, but this is far from true. Women, for example, were not *required* to make the journey to Jerusalem to celebrate the festivals (Deuteronomy 16:16). They *could*, and *often did*, but not when limited by pregnancy or small children, for example. In *The Essential Talmud*, Adin Steinsaltz writes, "The fact that women were not obliged to perform many of the positive precepts was regarded as an exemption rather than a ban. Men persisted in regarding themselves as the more fortunate sex, privileged to fulfill a greater number of precepts; this is attested to by the benediction recited each morning in which a man praises God for not having made him a woman" (p. 139).

rest of the Torah. These two commands are never said to replace the other commands, but all the other commandments can be integrated into these comprehensive summaries. The first of the *Two Great Commandments* contains a partial quotation from the *Sh'ma*. The *Sh'ma* is the most recited text in Judaism in both synagogue service and daily devotion.[205] Theologically, it emphasizes the unity of God. Practically, it commands the Hebrews to, "…Love the Lord your God with all your heart…" This first commandment is taken from Deuteronomy 6:5. The second commandment, "Love your neighbor as yourself," finds it origin in Leviticus 19:18.

The practice of summarizing and condensing the Law was not unique to Jesus:

> The sages referred to a comprehensive summary of Scripture as *kelal gadol batorah* (a great rule of Torah). Rabbi Akiva said that the most important summary statement in Scripture is, "You shall love your neighbor as yourself."[206]

Today we will look at *The Two Great Commandments*: loving God and loving others. Since it is impossible to obey the first without obeying the second, trying to separate them is a surgery we cannot perform. Even Christ refused to perform such a dissection. Although we cannot divide them when it comes to obedience, we can contemplate them individually and then reunite them for practice.

Vertical Love: Loving God

---

[205] "It is a major feature of the morning and evening prayer service…It is one of the two pillars…of Jewish prayer and worship" (David A. Rausch, *Building Bridges*, p. 239).
[206] David Bivin, *New Light on the Difficult Words of Jesus*, p. 86. Bivin, in turn, is quoting the *Sifra, Kedoshim to Lev. 19:18*.

I submit that Jesus' teachings about love find their origin in Deuteronomy (primarily), and that many of his statements about love are *Midrashim*.

Some might argue that Yeshua is not expositing the Deuteronomy texts, but simply dealing with the same *topic*. The mystery of inspiration negates the *demand* for an intentional, conscious connection on the part of New Testament authors. Since the same God inspired both Torah and the New Testament, this in itself *could* account for similarities.[207] I have concluded otherwise and operate under the theory that both Jesus and John do have the *First Testament* texts in mind. The fact that Yeshua freely quotes these verses suggests *Midrash* to me. The reader must decide matters for himself.

In my string of New Testament texts, I am including a verse from I John that also seems to be founded upon the Deuteronomy text – or perhaps Yeshua's *Midrash* whose source is the Deuteronomy text.

> *The First Covenant Transfer*

We can define vertical love as *our love for God in response to his prior love for us*. These Torah texts (Deuteronomy 6:5 and 7:6-11, ESV) bear upon vertical love:

> You shall love the LORD your God with all your heart and with all your soul and with all your might.
>
> For you are a people holy to the LORD your God. The LORD your God has chosen you to be a people for his treasured possession, out of all the peoples who are on the face of the earth. It was not because you were more in number than any other people

---

[207] I prefer to ascribe the conscious thought and intent of the human author as the norm in my view of verbal inspiration, particularly in didactic material; so I prefer to start with that assumption. Yet it is an assumption, and I freely admit that I could be wrong! God is God and I am not.

> that the LORD set his love on you and chose you, for you were the fewest of all peoples, but it is because the LORD loves you and is keeping the oath that he swore to your fathers, that the LORD has brought you out with a mighty hand and redeemed you from the house of slavery, from the hand of Pharaoh king of Egypt. Know therefore that the LORD your God is God, the faithful God who keeps covenant and steadfast love with those who love him and keep his commandments, to a thousand generations, and repays to their face those who hate him, by destroying them. He will not be slack with one who hates him. He will repay him to his face. You shall therefore be careful to do the commandment and the statutes and the rules that I command you today.

In the Deuteronomy 7 section, the verses imply that God *first* loved Abraham, Isaac, and Jacob – and then *transferred that love* to their descendents: "but it is because the LORD loves you and is keeping the oath that he swore to your fathers …"

From the creation account onward, God evidences a blanket love for all mankind. In the beginning, man was created in the image of God. In Genesis 9:1-17, God made a covenant with Noah and all his descendents, thus encompassing all mankind. The covenant itself places special value on human life. Though the race is fallen, men are still declared to be in the divine image. It is not that God has *no* love for mankind and only loves the descendents of Israel; it is, rather, that he has a special, unique love for Israel over and above his love for mankind. We might describe this as an "elective love."

The unique love God has for Israel is not completely a one-way street; it demands a response of love in return. The Israelites were expected to keep (obey) Yahweh's covenant as a response to his love. Refusing to keep his covenant is equivalent to scorning God's love, and thus provokes his wrath (7:10-11).

As poet William Congreve wrote of broken romantic love in the late 17th century, "Heav'n has no Rage, like Love to Hatred turn'd, Nor Hell a Fury, like a Woman scorn'd…" When God's love is scorned, he too is filled with rage. This rage, while expressed emotionally, is not solely emotional; it is the proper and expected consequence for violating his justice and holiness.

> ➢ *The Second (New) Covenant Transfer*

I believe these New Testament passages are related to the above texts:

> John 3:16 "For God so loved the world that he gave his one and only Son, that whoever believes in him shall not perish but have eternal life."
>
> John 3:36, "Whoever believes in the Son has eternal life, but whoever rejects the Son will not see life, for God's wrath remains on him."
>
> John 14:21,"Whoever has my commands and obeys them, he is the one who loves me. He who loves me will be loved by my Father, and I too will love him and show myself to him."
>
> I John 3:1, How great is the love the Father has lavished on us, that we should be called children of God! And that is what we are! The reason the world does not know us is that it did not know him.

The Father's love for the believer in Yeshua is likewise the result of a transfer, but this special love is transferred to us from the Father's love for his only Son. An additional text seems to make this clear, John 5:20-24 (ESV):

> "For the Father loves the Son and shows him all that he himself is doing. And greater works than these will he show him, so that you may marvel. For as the Father raises the dead and gives them life, so also the Son gives life to whom he will. The Father judges no one, but has given all judgment to the Son, that all may honor the Son, just as they honor the Father. Whoever does not honor the Son does not honor the Father who sent him. Truly, truly, I say to you, whoever hears my word and believes him

who sent me has eternal life. He does not come into judgment, but has passed from death to life."

The Scriptures describing the believer as "in Christ" or "in the beloved" suggest such a transfer.[208] The Father's love for the Son is transferred to us because we are "in Christ." If we honor Jesus, we automatically honor the Father. The Father does not condemn us if we have faith in the Son. In a similar sense, we are considered righteous because the Father considers the Son righteous, and we are in the Son.[209]

John 3:16 speaks of God's general love for the world, a love so profound that it resulted in the greatest grace gift of all time: the Father gave mankind his Son. In contrast, I John 3:1 announces a special love God has reserved for his own New Covenant people. This love extends above and beyond Yahweh's general love for mankind. This love is "lavished" upon us; the Father views regenerate believers as his tender children.

> How great is the love the Father has lavished on us, that we should be called children of God! And that is what we are! The reason the world does not know us is that it did not know him.

➤ Our Love Returned "Upward"

We are expected to return this love to the Father by means of obedience to him (cf. John 14:21 above). We are to demonstrate our love for God by obeying him. That obedience

---

[208] Ephesians 1:6 in the NASB reads, "to the praise of the glory of His grace, which He freely bestowed on us in the Beloved…"

[209] Romans 8:1 is one of many texts that teach this concept: "Therefore, there is now no condemnation for those who are in Christ Jesus…"

refers to the many specific commands of Scripture: worship, "proving" his will, making disciples, nurturing contentment, and meditating day and night on his Word. In a sense, this is how we love him as "Lord" (master).

Because God is personal, our love for Him should be personal. As is the case with human love, our love for God includes allegiance, faithfulness, mutual enjoyment, and relational development. We should love God as our friend, not merely as a functionary. Abraham is called the "friend of God,"[210] and the Christian will be the "companion" of Jesus Christ for eternity.[211] Yeshua clearly calls his disciples, "friends."[212] That friendship is anticipated to be mutual.

Although human self-discipline certainly affects the quality of our relationship to God, the motivation to love God is divinely driven. The fruit of the Spirit is love; this level of love does not originate as one of the "works of the flesh" (human nature), but results from the Spirit creating such a desire within us.[213] It is fair to say that all true believers love God, but it is also fair to say that the depth of our love for God varies – not only between believers, but within stages and eras of our own lives.

---

[210] James 2:23 (ESV), "and the Scripture was fulfilled that says, 'Abraham believed God, and it was counted to him as righteousness'—and he was called a friend of God."

[211] Notice that we are said to be the brothers and by implication in Hebrews, the companions of Jesus: Romans 8:29, "For those God foreknew he also predestined to be conformed to the likeness of his Son, that he might be the firstborn among many brothers…"; Hebrews 1:9, "You have loved righteousness and hated wickedness; therefore God, your God, has set you above your companions by anointing you with the oil of joy."

[212] See John 15:15.

[213] Galatians 5:22 and Philippians 2:13.

> *The Grim Destiny of Those Who Do Not Love God*

Those who scorn God's love by rejecting him will experience his wrath. John 3:36 explains (without apology): "Whoever believes in the Son has eternal life, but whoever rejects the Son will not see life, for *God's wrath remains* on him." This corresponds to Deuteronomy 7:10, "[The LORD] … repays to their face those who hate him, by destroying them…" Rejecting the Lord in both testaments brings Yahweh's wrath. The picture in John's Gospel is that God's wrath is already upon an individual by nature,[214] but the message of Messiah offers each of us life and release from that wrath. Those who pass by this opportunity *remain* under God's wrath. Thus mankind is born in a lost condition needing redemption. This is different from popular folk religion, which implies that an individual is born "found" and must do something particularly bad to become lost.[215]

Horizontal Love: Loving Others

It is impossible to love God without loving others, since God demands us to do so. It is possible to love others, however, without loving God. Sadly, many view Christian faith (and religion in general) as a means to such an end. Religious people frequently assert, "Well, what really matters is that we are all trying to make this world a better place." Our

---

[214] Ephesians 2:3 reads, "All of us also lived among them at one time, gratifying the cravings of our sinful nature and following its desires and thoughts. Like the rest, *we were by nature objects of wrath*."

[215] The way to harmonize this with the presentation in Deuteronomy is this: In Deuteronomy whether one is regenerate or not is exposed by his or her disposition toward following the LORD. Those responding to his love evidence a circumcised heart; thus obedience or disobedience flows from the spiritual disposition of the individual.

disagreement can shock others as we reply, "Making the world a better place is not the main goal of my faith." Indeed, those of us who believe we exist primarily to glorify God view our influence upon society (or mankind) as an important application of our faith, but not its focus. Our priorities are aimed God-ward, not man-ward. In our desire to serve God, we must care about humankind, for God demands it.[216] This is why Yeshua himself refused to reduce the Law down to only one command; it takes two.

How we arrive at the conviction that we must love others is crucial. The image of God within us craves to love others; even though our sin nature focuses upon self-interest, loving others is somewhat natural. It *feels* good to help others: God created us to be happiest when we give of ourselves, whether regenerate or not.

Jesus' followers must be careful to avoid the great humanism of *using* God to help mankind. God is not a means to an end – glorifying God is the end! We can, however, help mankind in Jesus' name for the purpose of glorifying God. When it comes to our personal relationship to God, *why* we do what we do is more important than *what* we do. The bottom line is not the bottom line.[217] This does not keep us from appreciating the work of others who do good things for wrong motives.[218]

> ➤ *Love of Man is Possible without Faith in God*

---

[216] Thus we do make the world a better place in the process.

[217] Proverbs 16:2 reads, "All a man's ways seem innocent to him, but motives are weighed by the LORD." See also I Corinthians 4:5.

[218] Philippians 1:18 is an example of this: "But what does it matter? The important thing is that in every way, whether from false motives or true, Christ is preached. And because of this I rejoice."

Some of the kindest and most reasonable people do not necessarily share our faith; even agnostics or atheists can be noted for their compassion. Teaching that the hallmark of the Christian is "love" does not imply that non-Christians cannot be loving people. This true story illustrates the point:

> When a man learned that an elderly woman could no longer buy her medicine and pay her rent, he came to her rescue. He took her into his home and treated her as if she were his mother. He gave her a bedroom, prepared the food for her meals, bought her medicine, and transported her whenever she needed medical attention. He continued to care for her when she could no longer do much for herself. I was amazed when I learned that this good man was a zealous atheist![219]

God expects us to exemplify love for others as a response to Christ's sacrificial love: "We love because he first loved us" (I John 4:19, ESV). Some translations insert understood pronouns, "We love *him* because he first loved *us*."[220] In such instances, the translators are supplying the word "him" and "us" in their attempt to make the sentence read smoothly. But the literal translation (as in the ESV) captures the true meaning: we love (perhaps "both God and men") because God's love came to us first in Christ. **Why** we love is what makes us unique, not merely that we love. Our human nature may motivate us to love others, but God's love intensifies and steers that love.

➤ *Horizontal Love According to Moses*

Leviticus 19:18 reads:

---

[219] "The Good Atheist," from the devotional booklet, *Our Daily Bread* for November 6, 2004; accessed at www.rbc.org on 2-17-10.
[220] Quoted from *The New King James Version*.

> Do not seek revenge or bear a grudge against one of your people, but *love your neighbor as yourself.* I am the LORD.

Deuteronomy 10:18-19 states:

> He defends the cause of the fatherless and the widow, and loves the alien, giving him food and clothing. And you are to love those who are aliens, for you yourselves were aliens in Egypt.

God commanded the people to "Love your neighbor." The question, "Who is my neighbor?" was a matter of debate between *Bet Hillel* and *Bet Shammai*, and Christ was caught in the crossfire of this debate. Yeshua did address this issue, as presented below.

As aforementioned, Harvey Falk argues a strong case that many of Jesus' disputes were with *Bet Shammai*, the dominant sect at the time of Yeshua's ministry. *Bet Shammai* accumulated a harsh track record; members of *Bet Shammai* were responsible for the death of 10 *Bet Hillel* disciples. They contracted the Zealots to do the dirty work. Although Hillel and Shammai themselves were civil toward one another, such was not always the case with their disciples.[221] This information may help us understand the intensity of these debates.

Falk postulates that *Bet Hillel* was driven to reach gentiles, perhaps even sending out missionaries for "evangelization."[222] As aforementioned, *Bet Hillel* taught that gentiles who turned from sin to the God of Israel and were willing to live by the seven Noahide

---

[221] Harvey Falk, *Jesus the Pharisee*, pp. 56-58.
[222] *Ibid.* pp. 30-33.

commands[223] would have a place in the "world to come." *Bet Shammai* taught that gentiles could not be saved, and he instituted rules that prevented Jews from interacting with gentiles[224] – rules vehemently opposed by *Bet Hillel*.[225]

> *Love of Aliens and Partial Converts*

We rarely hear discussion about the meaning the command to "love aliens." The horizontal love of which Moses spoke involves not only loving one's neighbor, but also loving aliens. Leviticus 19:34 states:

> The alien living with you must be treated as one of your native-born. Love him as yourself, for you were aliens in Egypt. I am the LORD your God.

How are we to understand the command to love aliens? Part of the difficulty involves understanding what the Hebrew term, *ger* signified. There are a variety of opinions on this subject, but I lean to the view of Falk:

> According to Scripture (Exodus 23:33), idolaters were not permitted to live in ancient Israel, lest they cause the people to sin. If a Gentile wished to settle there, he would

---

[223] "The nations of the world have been given a Divine code of conduct, the Seven Noachide Laws, which consist of six prohibitions against murder, robbery, idolatry, adultery, blasphemy, cruelty to animals – and one positive command, to establish a judicial system. These Seven Noachide Laws are general statements, which, with their ramifications and extensions, encompass countless details." ("The Rebbe Speaks on Noahide," www.noahide.org, accessed 2-17-10).

[224] "...the Shammaites proposed to prevent all communication between Jew and Gentile, by prohibiting the Jews from buying any article of food or drink from their heathen neighbors..." Competition and vast differences in Torah interpretation between these groups was so massive that the *Talmud* says, "The one Law has become two laws" (Tosef., ag. ii. 9; Sanh. 88b; Soṭah 47b)." [source: Jastrow, Marcus and Mendelsohn, S., *The Jewish Encyclopedia*, "Bet Hillel and Bet Shammai," www.Jewishencyclopedia.com, accessed 2-17-10].

[225] Harvey Falk, *Jesus the Pharisee*, pp. 56-58.

appear before three learned men, accept the Noahide Laws, and would then be permitted to settle with the status of a *Ger Toshav*.[226]

Craigie Comments:

> The resident alien was a foreigner who resided with the Israelites under their protection, and though he was not equal in all respects to the Israelites, under the law he was treated as they were.[227]

We have already dealt with the various levels of conversion for a gentile toward Judaism in chapter two. This includes the "alien."[228] So is the love for an alien different than the love for a neighbor? Jesus simplifies matters (as we shall see below) by expanding the command to love our neighbor as including loving others in general – neighbor or alien.

> ➢ *Horizontal Love According to Yeshua*

The Golden Rule is perhaps the most widely accepted definition of what it means to love others. In Luke 10:31, Yeshua states, "Do unto others as you would have them do unto you." The idea of putting yourself in another's shoes suggests empathy.

---

[226] See Harvey Falk, *Jesus the Pharisee*, pp. 26-27. Falk references these *Talmud* portions and sources to his comment: *Sanhedrin* 105a, 56a-59b; *Rosh-Ha-Shanah* 17a; *Maimonides, Issurei Biah* 14:7, *Avodat Kochavim* 62a.

[227] P.C. Craigie, *The Book of Deuteronomy*, p. 98.

[228] See *The Enduring Paradox*, (Dr. John Fischer, editor), p. 178. In chapter two, I pointed out that Patrice Fischer reconstructs a possible Second Temple paradigm about conversion to Judaism and its various levels. This would be from a *Bet Hillel* perspective, based upon the foundation we have laid. A pagan idolater could become a *Gerey toshev* (alien/foreigner) if he wanted to be righteous; he would acknowledge the one true God of Israel and align his life under the Noachide commands. If he wanted to go further, he could become a *Gerey hasha'ir* (God fearer). In addition to the Noachide commands, he would observe the Sabbath, eat *kosher*, and participate in synagogue learning. If he wanted to become a full convert to Judaism, he would be circumcised (if a man), be immersed (both genders), have a sacrifice made in the Temple, and pay Temple tax.

Hillel expressed a similar thought, but Hillel's statement is more about what you *don't* do to another: "What is painful to you, do not do unto others."[229] What Jesus does is to make love *proactive*. Love is not only about avoiding harm. Although Hillel's statement is not as rich as Yeshua's, *Bet Hillel* placed a high premium upon loving others. Because of this, *Bet Hillel* did a lot of thinking about how love looked in practical settings. Rabbi Akiva, who identified with *Bet Hillel* states:

> Whatever you hate to have done unto you, do not do to your neighbor; wherefore do not hurt him; do not speak ill of him; do not reveal his secrets to others; let his honor and his property be as dear to thee as thine own.[230]

Jesus often found himself at odds with *Bet Shammai*. As mentioned in a previous chapter, the exception was Christ's agreement with *Bet Shammai* on the divorce issue. *Bet Hillel* espoused compassion toward all, *Bet Shammai* discouraged compassion toward non-Jews. Modern Judaism and almost all of the Talmud reflect the perspective of *Bet Hillel,* but *Bet Shammai* was the major influence in Israel when Yeshua walked the earth. The Parable of the Good Samaritan supports the spirit of *Bet Hillel* and would irritate members of *Bet Shammai*.

➢ *The Good Samaritan*

Luke 10:25-37 (ESV) presents one of the best known parables Jesus taught:

> And behold, a lawyer stood up to put him to the test, saying, "Teacher, what shall I do to inherit eternal life?" He said to him, "What is written in the Law? How do you read

---

[229] *Talmud, Shabbat* 31a
[230] *Midrash Avot de Rabbi Natan*

it?" And he answered, "You shall love the Lord your God with all your heart and with all your soul and with all your strength and with all your mind, and your neighbor as yourself." And he said to him, "You have answered correctly; do this, and you will live."

But he, desiring to justify himself, said to Jesus, "And who is my neighbor?" Jesus replied, "A man was going down from Jerusalem to Jericho, and he fell among robbers, who stripped him and beat him and departed, leaving him half dead. Now by chance a priest was going down that road, and when he saw him he passed by on the other side. So likewise a Levite, when he came to the place and saw him, passed by on the other side. But a Samaritan, as he journeyed, came to where he was, and when he saw him, he had compassion. He went to him and bound up his wounds, pouring on oil and wine. Then he set him on his own animal and brought him to an inn and took care of him. And the next day he took out two denarii and gave them to the innkeeper, saying, 'Take care of him, and whatever more you spend, I will repay you when I come back.' Which of these three, do you think, proved to be a neighbor to the man who fell among the robbers?" He said, "The one who showed him mercy." And Jesus said to him, "You go, and do likewise."

> *The Samaritans Were the Ultimate Aliens*

The hostility between the Jews and the Samaritans was well known.[231] John, in his Gospel (4:9b), makes the point simply: "For Jews do not associate with Samaritans." The

---

[231] The "Samaritans" appear often in the Scripture: the Good Samaritan, the woman at the well, and the command to preach the Gospel in Samaria (Acts 1:8). Some Pharisees accused Christ of having a demon and being a Samaritan himself (John 8:48). Who were these mysterious Samaritans?

The nation of Israel, even when united, was the union of the North (the majority of the tribes) and the South (Judah, the largest tribe). The union was always shaky. For years even King David ruled only over Judah—until the Northern Tribes elected to join his confederacy. When David's grandson (Rehoboam) took the throne, the northern tribes broke rank. They appointed their own king (Jeroboam) and severed ties to the South. This Northern confederacy was sometimes called, "Samaria."

When the Assyrians conquered this Northern Kingdom in 722 BC, they imported gentiles into the land of Samaria and deported many Israelites. Since the northern Israelites had long ago resorted to idolatry, it was natural for the various people groups to intermarry, forming the people group referred to as "Samaritans." Eventually, a Samaritan form of monotheistic Judaism prevailed. The Samaritans adjusted the Torah and rewrote history, claiming that they were the pure race, while asserting that the Jews (Judeans) were the mixed race.

historical reasons for this are numerous and complex, but I would suggest that neither side was innocent; the hatred was mutual. We might compare it to a family in which legitimately born brothers had an illegitimate half-brother whom they despise, while the illegitimate brother resents his siblings precisely because they have rejected him. Although it seems evident that the Jewish people as a whole avoided contact with the Samaritans, some Jews – particularly *Bet Hillel* – probably held a higher opinion of them than *Bet Shammai*.[232]

Like Jesus, many rabbis and disciples did not agree with every point from a single school. This particular law expert, on the one hand, summarizes the way to salvation (and a

---

Many of the Judeans were deported to Babylon (beginning in 606 BC through 586) after Babylon had defeated the Southern Kingdom. They began returning to Jerusalem seventy years later (536, under Ezra). They began to rebuild the temple and the city.

The Samaritans (referred to as "the people of the land) opposed this; in their alteration of the Torah, they proclaimed that Mount Gerizim was God's chosen location for the central sanctuary, not Jerusalem. Nehemiah tells us they used red tape as a tactic to inhibit the construction of Jerusalem's walls; the animosity grew over the centuries.

Both groups hated and went out of their way to irritate one another. For example, the Jews would signal the beginning of a holy day based on the sunset in Jerusalem. The Rabbi there would give the sign, and fires would be immediately lit from mountaintop to mountaintop throughout the entire region. The holy day had begun. The Samaritans, however, would sometimes light false fires just to confound the Jews.

Modern Judaism recognizes the full Jewishness of the Samaritan people, several thousand of whom still live in Israel (and have all along). Their Rabbis are considered fully accredited; they are stricter than even Orthodox Jews. [See "Samaritans," *The International Standard Bible Encyclopedia*, Vol. 4, 1988, pp.303-304 and *The Jewish Encyclopedia* "Samaritans" by A. Cowley, Joseph Jacobs, and Henry Minor Huxley, www.jewishencyclopedia.com, accessed 3-01-10].

[232] Harvey Falk writes, "His [Jesus'] view of the Samaritans seems to compare with that of R. Simeon ben Gamaliel (Hullin 4a) – a great grandson of Hillel – who held that the Samaritans were more observant of the commandments they had adopted than the Jews themselves. R. Eliezer of Bet Shammai held (ibid.) that the Samaritans could not be trusted in the observance of the commandments" (*Jesus the Pharisee*, p. 69). On the dominance of Bet Shammai over all of Judaism at the time of Yeshua, see Falk, pp. 93-96.

summary of the law) as the Two Great Commandments,[233] an answer we might expect from *Bet Hillel*. Yet his question, "Who is my neighbor?" implies he favored the more isolationist view of *Bet Shammai*.

Yeshua develops a story which surprisingly presents a Samaritan as the hero, while the story's priest and Levite are painted negatively. Since many lower-level priests and Levites (and scribes) were followers of *Bet Shammai* (and sometimes Zealots), this might further suggest that Messiah is chatting with a scribe who is sympathetic with *Bet Shammai*.[234]

At the end of the parable, Yeshua asks the scribe, "Which of these three, do you think, proved to be a neighbor to the man who fell among the robbers?"

We can almost hear the hesitation as the scribe is forced to recite the only sensible response: "The one who showed him mercy." Thus Jesus makes the point than an alien – even a despised Samaritan – can fulfill the role of a neighbor. Every human being deserves to be treated as a human being.

---

[233] Many of us in the evangelical camp might ask, "Why didn't Jesus simply say one could not be saved (inherit eternal life) by law-keeping? After all, salvation is by grace alone through faith alone in Christ alone." The answer is that Jesus (and sometimes Paul, Peter, or John) does not distinguish between cause and correlation. Since loving God and others is the result and evidence of regeneration, there is no attempt made to distinguish the fruit from the tree that produces the fruit. This is a frustration to modern, western logic, but we must recognize that there is more than one way to reason. We have seen similar cases already in this book, for example Deuteronomy 5:29, 10:12-17, 11:13, and 30:6. Whose responsibility is what? The best reconciliation is that those whom God regenerates are guaranteed to exemplify the fruit He demands.

[234] These two schools were so far apart that the *Talmud* describes it as an era when "the Torah became two Torahs" (*Sanhedrin* 88b).

Special Considerations: A Rabbit Trail Concerning Love

> *How Does Love Differ?*

Although Yeshua taught us to love our neighbors, even if they are of a different race or creed, the love we have for others varies. Our love varies in both intensity and nature. Ancient New Testament Biblical Greek has about a 6,000-word vocabulary.[235] Common English has a vocabulary of over 75,000 words (not including technical or rare terms). English has by far the broadest vocabulary of any language; my three-volume dictionary lists over 450,000 words!

As a result of such a massive vocabulary, the English language includes nuances of meaning that eclipse those offered by any other language, including New Testament (*koine*) Greek.

The New Testament word for love, *agape* (or its verbal form, *agapao*), is a prime example. Contrary to popular belief, the word *agape* is not unique to the New Testament.[236] Its verb form (*agapao*) was used in common Greek language much as we would use our English "love." In the Greek translation of the Hebrew Old Testament (LXX) book of Genesis, for example, Jacob is said to *agapao* Esau's stew. The other

---

[235] There are 5,393 words used in the Greek New Testament (see "Wordbase Greek," http://greek.kihlman.eu/, accessed 3-2-10).

[236] Leon Morris argues that the noun form, *agape*, was used only rarely in Greek, but of the verb form, *agapao*, he writes, "Perhaps I should make it clear that the newness is in the noun, not the verb…The verb *agapao* was used quite frequently in pre-Christian times, but when the Christians used it they gave it a deeper meaning" [*Testaments of Love*, pp. 126-127]. The point is that Christians MADE the word "*agape*" special, but that special, deeper meaning evolved AFTER Pentecost and would have little bearing on the Gospels.

Greek word for love, *phileo*, is used more commonly in Greek, but it is used sparingly in the New Testament.[237] *Phileo* suggests "brotherly love," a clear and clean meaning.[238] *Agape* can mean anything from "niceness" (as in 1 Corinthians 4:21) to the self-sacrificing love of God (John 3:16) and the spectrum in between.

In all languages, words vary in meaning and are honed by context. This is true with the broadly used words for love. We do not love our enemy in the same way in which a man loves his wife. The distinction is not determined by the word *agape* or *phileo*, but by the context. Let me suggest some key differences between varieties of love we typically encounter.

The love of God for us is the love of redemption.[239] God the Son became a man to die for our sins. We might call this "sacrificial love." **A man is to love his wife** in a way that is also sacrificial, but there is an additional element in the love between spouses. We might call this love a *blending love* as two attempt to function as one; in Genesis 2:21-22, the woman was removed from man; in marriage, she returns to his side (Genesis 2:24-25). Affectionate **Parent-child** love is the love *du jour* in 1 Thessalonians 2:7-8:

---

[237] The verb form, *phileo,* is used 25 times in the New Testament, while the verb form, *agapao*, is used 143 times [*The New NIV Exhaustive Concordance*, p. 1803 and p. 1673, respectively]. Colin Brown, speaking of *koine'* Greek, writes, "*phileo* is the most commonly used word, indicating a general attraction toward a person or thing" [*The New International Dictionary of New Testament Theology*, Volume 2, p. 538].
[238] *Ibid*.
[239] Romans 5:8 makes the point: "But God demonstrates his own love for us in this: While we were still sinners, Christ died for us."

> But we were gentle among you, like a mother caring for her little children. We loved you so much that we were delighted to share with you not only the gospel of God but our lives as well, because you had become so dear to us.

We can call this a *bonding love*. The parent-child bond changes as the child matures, and so does the nature of that love. Then there is the **love between siblings**. We can call this *a supporting love*. **The love between close friends** was exemplified between David and Jonathan and well known within military. We might describe this as *the love of camaraderie*. **Fellow Christians** are to be known for their love one for another. We might call this *fellowship love*. 1 Corinthians 13 is probably addressing this slant on love. **Loving our neighbor** demonstrates the *love of concern*. Showing **love to our enemy** would be the *love of duty*, a love that often runs contrary to emotion. These loves are not mutually exclusive.

> ➤ *Peter's Restoration and Plays on the Word "Love."*

In John 21:1-25 Jesus confronted Peter with the question, "Do you love me?" thrice. The obvious implication is that Jesus is undoing Peter's triple denial of Yeshua before his Passion. The scholarly Leon Morris writes:

> In a most instructive incident, Jesus talks with Peter by the lake, asking three times whether that disciple loves him.... Discussions often center on the fact that twice Jesus uses the verb agapao (αγαπαο) in his question, to be met each time by Peter's use of phileo (φιλεο) in his answer. Then in the third question Jesus uses Peter's word and the apostle retains it in his reply. But the significant thing is surely not so much the variation in the verb, but the fact that Jesus is speaking about love at all. Peter's position in the apostolic band must have been at least dubious in light of his threefold

denial of Jesus. This incident, in which Peter three times affirms his love for his Lord in the presence of the other apostles, must be seen as a reinstatement...." [240]

Jesus asks Peter twice, "Do you *agapao* me?" And Peter answers, "Yes, I *phileo* you," until, on the third time, Christ asks, "Do you *phileo* me?" and Peter responds the same way as the other two times, "Yes, I *phileo* you."

I agree with Morris that the *main* concept is reinstatement, not the Greek words.[241] But the fact that the words vary as they do is still significant. Was Peter being stubborn? What was happening here?

What few consider is that Jesus and Peter did not converse in Greek. They never actually mouthed the words *phileo* or *agapao* to one another. Although the authors of Scripture were inspired, they were still translating the words of Yeshua from Mishnaic Hebrew into Greek. This is in contrast to the epistles, Acts, and Revelation, which were completely composed in Greek. This inter-language issue requires detective work as we attempt to move from the written Greek into the spoken Hebrew.

The Hebrew word Jesus first used could have used was *ahebh*. Generally speaking, this word can be used for all kinds of love.[242]

---

[240] Morris, Leon, *Testaments of Love*, pp. 180-181; Harvey Falk connects the priesthood to the Zealots and to Bet Shammai (*Jesus the Pharisee*, pp. 120-121).
[241] Morris, pp. 180-81.
[242] According to Harris, Waltke, and Archer, the word *aheb* means "love, like, be in love, lovely." They comment, "There is little variation in the basic meaning of this verb. The intensity of the meaning ranges from God's infinite affections for his people to the carnal appetites of a lazy glutton" [*Theological Wordbook of the Old Testament, Volume 1*, p. 14].

Peter may have answered with the Hebrew word *hesedh*, which means a steadfast love, a deep, lasting affection that is based upon relationship.[243] This word is often used of God's faithful love for those under His covenant, but can refer to mercy or goodwill.

If my theory is correct, Jesus may have been asking, "Peter, do you love me?" and Peter responded, "Yes, Lord. I love you steadfastly, based on our relationship." This would be especially meaningful since Peter had not been steadfast during his time of denial. When Jesus finally uses Peter's word, He was acknowledging that Peter was restored. What a beautiful example of love in action.

God wants us to love Him, but He wants us to love Him steadfastly. Steadfast love always trumps fickle love.

Conclusion

Loving God and loving others is an important priority for one who would follow Jesus. That love, however, needs to be a carefully reasoned love, defined by the Word of God and not by popular viewpoints. Why we pursue love is crucial: Christian love begins with our relationship to God and our desire to honor him first of all. God is not the means to an end (making the world a better place), but God's glory is the end.

---

[243] "The general English renderings for the word in the A.V. are: kindness, mercy, pity, favour, goodness, and lovingkindness. It is often found united with righteousness, faithfulness, truth, compassion, and other divine qualities" [Robert A. Girdlestone, *Synonyms of the Old Testament*, p. 111].

Chapter 8: The Great Prophet
(Deuteronomy 18:15-19 with John 10:1-30)

I love a cliffhanger. As a boy, I remember watching *Flash Gordon* on Saturday morning via our old black and white television set. Even in the 1960's, those vintage 1930's serials held my attention; each episode ended with Flash on the verge of disaster. Somehow, in the next episode, Flash would manage to escape impending death!

The First Testament leaves us with a few vintage cliffhangers of a different kind. We find ourselves anticipating a number of mysterious personages who were prophesied to surface in the future. We are told that Elijah would return before the great and terrible "day of the Lord."[244] We read numerous texts that predict the Messiah. The Messianic prophecies seem to follow two tracks: a lamb-like Messiah associated with suffering, and a lion-like Messiah who would rule the world. To harmonize these two distinct tracks, later Jews postulated the idea of two Messiahs. One Messiah would be a descendent of Joseph, (Jacob's favored son),[245] and he would experience suffering. The other Messiah would be the descendent of David and reign over the earth.[246] The Christian solution was simpler: the one Messiah – the descendent of David – would appear twice. Thus Yeshua

---

[244] Malachi 4:5

[245] Matthew 2:33b reads, ""He will be called a Nazarene." Since Nazareth was north, in the part of Israel sometimes called "Joseph," there may be a possible ancient connection between this location and the later idea that one Messiah would descend from Joseph.

[246] Michael Brown, *Answering Jewish Objections to Jesus, Volume 2*, p. 212.

came the first time as *The Lamb of God*, and we believe he will return the second time as *The Lion of the Tribe of Judah*.

Another shadowy prophecy in the *First Testament* leaves us anticipating a Moses-like Prophet (Deuteronomy 18:15-19). While Christians generally recognize Jesus as the fulfillment of messianic prediction, few contemplate Jesus as this Moses-like prophet. Although Christ never directly *stated* that he himself was the expected prophet, it is my contention that he *did imply* that he was this prophet. In contrast to Yeshua's indirect implications, Peter boldly stated that Yeshua *is* the predicted prophet, as demonstrated below (Acts 3:21-23).

John the Baptist and the Moses-like Prophet

The Jewish leaders in the first-century did not know how to interpret the ministry of John (Yochanan) the Baptist. Israel's spiritual leadership sent a delegation to investigate Yochanan and to drill him with a barrage of questions, a few of which are recorded in The Gospel According to (the Apostle) John.[247] John 1:19-21 summarizes:

> Now this was John's testimony when the Jews of Jerusalem sent priests and Levites to ask him who he was. He did not fail to confess, but confessed freely, "I am not the Christ."
>
> They asked him, "Then who are you? Are you Elijah?"
>
> He said, "I am not."
>
> "Are you the Prophet?"
>
> He answered, "No."

---

[247] These representatives were probably sent by the Jewish ruling body, the Sanhedrin.

Yochanan clearly denied being the Messiah, Elijah, *and* the Prophet. He is merely the predicted "voice" crying out in the wilderness.[248] The question we will examine is, "Was Yeshua the specific Prophet Moses predicted?" A related question is, "If so, did Jesus present himself (even if subtly) as not only as Messiah, but likewise as the long-anticipated prophet?"

The Responsibility of the People to Hear and Obey the Prophet

In Deuteronomy 18:15-19, we are introduced to the prediction of a coming prophet:

> The LORD your God will raise up for you a prophet like me from among your own brothers. You must listen to him. For this is what you asked of the LORD your God at Horeb on the day of the assembly when you said, "Let us not hear the voice of the LORD our God nor see this great fire anymore, or we will die."

> The LORD said to me: "What they say is good. I will raise up for them a prophet like you from among their brothers; I will put my words in his mouth, and he will tell them everything I command him. If anyone does not listen to my words that the prophet speaks in my name, I myself will call him to account."

The Septuagint (LXX) version ends verse 19 this way, "And whatever man shall not harken to whatsoever words the prophet shall speak in my name, I will take vengeance on him."[249] This is an important clue to pre-Christian Jewish interpretation of the phrase, "call him to account." When God "calls to account" it was understood as equivalent to receiving God's wrath. The variant of this passage in Acts is not based on the LXX, but is a paraphrase (perhaps a Targum) interpreting God's vengeance as being administered by

---

[248] See John 1:23 and Isaiah 40:3.
[249] Sir Lancelot C.L Brenton, *The Septuagint with Apocrypha: Greek and English*, p. 256.

the agency of due Jewish legal process, thus revealing yet another interpretation of what it means to be "called into account."

The following points about this prophet surface in the above-cited text: (1) ignoring this prophet equates to ignoring God, (2) the people must listen to him (i.e., hear and obey him), (3) the words he speaks are God's words, and (4) those who reject him will experience God's condemnation.

That fourth point is particularly interesting if we view it from an opposite perspective. If those who refuse to listen to the Moses-like prophet are condemned, then one possible opposite is that those who *do* listen to him are saved (delivered or passed over) when it comes to God's judgment. I concede that other alternatives are logically possible. For example, individuals who follow this prophet might be condemned for other reasons. Yet this fourth point might not be conceptually far from, "If you believe him, you are saved; if you reject him, you are lost."

One Prophet or a String of Prophets?

While commenting on this text, Bernard Schneider writes,

> …Who is this prophet? The answer is both simple and complex. It is simple because the New Testament indicates that this prophet is Christ (cf. Acts 3:20-23). The answer is complex in that the whole line of prophets seems to be included.[250]

---

[250] Bernard N. Schneider, *Deuteronomy: A Favored Book By Jesus*, pp. 107-108.

The word "prophet" is singular, yet many interpreters (like Schneider) take it to refer to the entire class of prophetic sages sent by Yahweh.[251] Whatever these scholars' hermeneutical skills, the John 1:19-21 passage cited above indicates that at least some first century Jews were expecting a *single* prophet to fulfill Moses' prediction. Indeed, *no other prophet has been truly Moses-like.* Elijah and Elisha worked a number of significant miracles, but not on par with those of Moses who delivered an entire nation out of slavery. There is no clear evidence that Elijah and Elisha had an amazing teaching ministry, as did Moses. Other prophets – for instance Isaiah – did a lot of teaching and prophesying, but did not work many (or any) miracles. On the other hand, Yeshua had to sometimes take a reprieve from the multitudes crowding him. Why did they crowd him? The answer is obvious: because of the voluminous healings he performed.[252] When it comes to miracle-working, only Jesus surpasses Moses. Amazingly, more great miracles are in store when Christ returns.[253]

Like Moses, Yeshua was born during a dark time within Israel's history. Like Moses, he escaped death as an infant. Messiah's Moses-like humility is particularly noteworthy. Moses is described as, "… a very humble man, more humble than anyone else on the face of the earth." In Matthew 11:29, Yeshua proclaims himself to be humble. We do not normally think of a humble person as one who would broadcast his own humility, but

---

[251] For example, see P.C. Craigie, *The Book of Deuteronomy*, p. 262; he, in turn, cites G. A. Smith.
[252] Mark 3:7-10 and Matthew 4:23-25 demonstrate the numerous nature of his miracles.
[253] See Zechariah 12-14 for a taste of these.

Jesus could do so because he *truly* was humble and mentioning his humility involved no pride: "Take my yoke upon you and learn from me, for I am gentle and humble in heart, and you will find rest for your souls."[254] Perhaps Christ mentioned his own humility to align himself with the quality for which Moses was famous, coupling himself to Moses.

Moses offered to be cut off for the sake of his people and Jesus intentionally purposed to give his life a ransom for many – and *he actually was cut off* for his own.[255]

John 6:14-15 further implies that the Jewish people were expecting one special prophet, and some concluded that Yeshua was he. After Jesus miraculously fed the multitude, we join the action midstream:

> After the people saw the miraculous sign that Jesus did, they began to say, "*Surely this is the Prophet who is to come into the world.*" Jesus, knowing that they intended to come and make him king by force, withdrew again to a mountain by himself.

Please note that the Yeshua's Jewish followers combined the idea of a King-Messiah with that of the expected Prophet. Thus this crowd anticipated the Christian teaching that Jesus was *both* the Prophet and the Messiah.

The Jews held the Torah in highest esteem and viewed Moses with unique honor because of his association with the transmission of the Torah. Thus only the Messiah himself

---

[254] Matthew 11:29

[255] In Exodus 32:32, Moses prayed to God and offered, "But now, please forgive their sin—but if not, then blot me out of the book you have written." See also Isaiah 53:8 where the Lord's Servant (the Messiah) is predicted to be "cut off." See also Daniel 9:26.

could match such a dispensation.[256] Only the Messiah *could* play in the same league with the Torah! Thus, logically, the Messiah becomes even more potent in authority if he is both Messiah and Prophet.

David Bivin points out an ancient Jewish tradition stating Messiah is greater than Moses:

> It is written, "Who are you, O great mountain? Before Zerubbabel you will become level ground" [Zech 4:7]. What is "Who are you, O great mountain"? This is the King Messiah. And why is he called a "great mountain"? Because he is greater that the patriarchs…elevated beyond Abraham, exalted above Moses and superior to the ministering angels.[257]

Jewish Diversity of Opinion: Was the Prophet also the Messiah?

As demonstrated in previous chapters, Jewish beliefs were only uniform in several key areas (the Oneness of God, the truth of the Torah, the Feasts, eating kosher, etc.). When it came to defining who this prophet would be, the sages held a variety of views.

> ➢ *The View that Jeremiah or Another Prophet Would Be Resurrected*

John Gill documents how some rabbis suggested that Jeremiah was the predicted Prophet. Gill wrote that Jeremiah was the one "…whom some of the Jews have thought to be the

---

[256] *The Jewish Encyclopedia* (www.jewishencyclopedia.com) article on "Torah" documents that the Jews believe that the Torah was created 2,000 years before the world; most Christians have no idea of the extreme reverence in which the Jews hold the Torah.
[257] Here, David Bivin in *New Light on the Difficult Words of Jesus* (p. 135) is quoting *Tanhuma, Toledot 134-138*.

prophet Moses spoke of, in Deuteronomy 18:15 and expected that he would appear about the time of the Messiah."[258]

Other rabbis believed that several great prophets would be resurrected when the Messiah came.[259] That may explain why Herod believed that Jesus was a resurrected John the Baptist [260] (who was considered a prophet by the people[261]).

Understanding these Second Temple beliefs helps us make sense of the popular Jewish assumptions we read about in the Gospels. In Luke's Gospel, when Jesus asks his disciples who people thought he was, they replied in Luke 19:19: "'John the Baptist, and others say Elijah; but others, that one of the prophets of old has risen again.'" Although Elijah never experienced death, John the Baptist had died and so had the prophets; the idea that resurrected prophets would appear in the era of the Messiah was obviously a common belief at the time![262]

> *The View that the Prophet Was Separate from the Messiah*

---

[258] See John Gill's comments on John 1:21, www.studylight.org, accessed 3-24-10; his source: Baal Hatturim in Deut. xviii. 15. Tzeror Hammor, fol. 127. 4. & 143. 4. Siphre in Jarchi in Jer. i. 5.
[259] John Lightfoot, *Commentary on the New Testament from the Talmud and Hebraica, Vol. 3*, p. 243
[260] Matthew 14:1-2, "At that time Herod the tetrarch heard the reports about Jesus, and he said to his attendants, 'This is John the Baptist; he has risen from the dead! That is why miraculous powers are at work in him.'"
[261] Matthew 14:5
[262] Matthew 27:52-53 is probably tied into this expectation: "The tombs broke open and the bodies of many holy people who had died were raised to life. They came out of the tombs, and after Jesus' resurrection they went into the holy city and appeared to many people." This is certainly one of the more mysterious passages of Scripture, but it could be that the Jewish anticipation of the resurrection of some Old Covenant prophets was accurate. We do not know if these "holy ones" ascended into heaven with resurrection bodies or returned to their graves. Perhaps we will learn more about this some day.

The apocryphal book of I Maccabees (14:41) suggests that the Jews in the centuries before Jesus were expecting this Prophet to surface:

> The Jewish people and their priest have, therefore, made the following decisions. Simon shall be their permanent leader and high priest until a true prophet arises.

As evidenced above in the portion from John's Gospel, some Jews either viewed the Prophet as distinct from the Messiah or were non-committal on the issue.

> ➤ *The View that the Prophet and Messiah Were One in the Same*

Michael L. Brown, referring to John J. Collins, comments:

> Collins suggests, however, that according to some key texts from the Dead Sea Scrolls, "the Messiah, whom heaven and earth will obey, is an anointed eschatological prophet, either Elijah or a prophet like Elijah."[263]

This text demonstrates the viewpoint that Messiah and the Prophet is one and the same person, whether Elijah or not.

> ➤ *The Clear Second Testament Teaching: Yeshua is the Foretold Prophet*

Acts 3:21-23 settles matters:

> He [Jesus] must remain in heaven until the time comes for God to restore everything, as he promised long ago through his holy prophets. For Moses said, "The Lord your God will raise up for you a prophet like me from among your own people; you must listen to everything he tells you. Anyone who does not listen to him will be completely cut off from among his people."

---

[263] Michael J. Brown in *Answering Jewish Objections to Jesus, Volume 3*, p. 197 cites John J. Collins from *The Scepter and the Star: The Messiahs of the Dead Sea Scrolls and Other Ancient Literature*, p. 116.

Peter states that the Deuteronomy prophecy of a Moses-like prophet was fulfilled completely and totally in Jesus Christ. From a question and answer viewpoint, the Christian has a no-spin answer: Jesus did fulfill the prophecy of the Moses-like prophet.

Did Yeshua Present Himself As the Prophet?

In John 5:46, Yeshua probably claimed to be the Prophet Moses predicted, "If you believed Moses, you would believe me, for he wrote about me." Still, Christ did not actually use the term, "The Prophet."

Although Jesus never did mouth the words that he was the anticipated Prophet (in contrast to his clear claims to be the Messiah),[264] *he expected to be obeyed as though he were that Prophet*, just as Moses expected to be obeyed. Most of us who are fluent in John's Gospel[265] can readily detect passages in that Gospel in which Jesus demands similar compliance. Jesus viewed himself as possessing the *prerogatives* of the expected Moses-like Prophet. This suggests that he believed that he was the Prophet.

---

[264] During his trial, Jesus' answer to the question, "Are you the King of the Jews" is one of clear affirmation, "You have said so," an emphatic "yes." But agenda-driven skeptics often refuse to bridge the chasm between literal translation and dynamic meaning if it suits their purposes. An irrefutable claim to Jesus being the Messiah is made in John 4:25-26, "The woman said to him, "I know that Messiah is coming (he who is called Christ). When he comes, he will tell us all things." Jesus said to her, "I who speak to you am he." If one chooses not to believe in Jesus as Messiah, that is his or her choice; but let no one deny that the Gospels teach that Jesus claimed to be the Messiah.

[265] Some authorities do not consider John's Gospel as historically reliable as the synoptics; this is unfortunate. The oldest Gospel (or New Testament) fragments are of John's Gospel, the *John Rylands Papyrus*; this fragment is dated from the first half of the second century. [source: *Introduction to New Testament Textual Criticism* by Harold Greenlee, p. 34]. Whereas the synoptics are probably compilations of memorized tractates, John probably wrote his Gospel to supplement what the synoptics omitted, in this author's opinion.

Recall the admonition to *listen* to the Prophet as stated in the Deuteronomy text above.

From John 10:1-5, 8, 11, 14-15, 25-30, we observe that Yeshua's sheep prove themselves true *by listening to* (hearing and obeying) him:

> "I tell you the truth, the man who does not enter the sheep pen by the gate, but climbs in by some other way, is a thief and a robber. The man who enters by the gate is the shepherd of his sheep. The watchman opens the gate for him, and the sheep listen to his voice. He calls his own sheep by name and leads them out. When he has brought out all his own, he goes on ahead of them, and his sheep follow him because they know his voice. But they will never follow a stranger; in fact, they will run away from him because they do not recognize a stranger's voice... All who ever came before me were thieves and robbers, but the sheep did not listen to them.
>
> "…I am the good shepherd. The good shepherd lays down his life for the sheep…"I am the good shepherd; I know my sheep and my sheep know me— just as the Father knows me and I know the Father—and I lay down my life for the sheep."
>
> …Jesus answered, "I did tell you, but you do not believe. The miracles I do in my Father's name speak for me, but you do not believe because you are not my sheep. My sheep listen to my voice; I know them, and they follow me. I give them eternal life, and they shall never perish; no one can snatch them out of my hand. My Father, who has given them to me, is greater than all; no one can snatch them out of my Father's hand. I and the Father are one."

> ➢ *The Prophet as a Shepherd*

It is interesting that Yeshua used the imagery of a shepherd and sheep. Consider that Moses, the prototype of the Prophet, had actually been a shepherd in Midian for forty years. Moses became the shepherd of Israel,[266] and Jesus uses similar imagery for himself.

---

[266] Isaiah 63:11

The Rabbis interpreted the "three shepherds" of Zechariah to refer to Moses, Miriam, and Aaron:

> When Aaron died, the pillar of cloud left. Still, both the well and the pillar of cloud were returned for the sake of Moses; but when Moses died, everything vanished, as it is written [Zechariah, xi. 8]: "And I removed the three shepherds in one month." Did then Moses, Aaron, and Miriam die in the same month? Did not Moses die in Adar, Aaron in Abh, and Miriam in Nissan? Therefore [we] infer from that passage that the three gifts which were given to Israel vanished in the same month that Moses died.[267]

The term "shepherd" is used throughout the *First Testament* of teachers/leaders (both good and evil) and of the Messiah's reign.[268] By calling himself "The Good Shepherd," Jesus was not merely claiming to be "a" good shepherd, but "The" Good Shepherd. Did his audience understand him to be thus calling himself "The Prophet?" Perhaps some did.

Eternal life and escaping judgment

In the John 10 text cited above, we see that the Good Shepherd provides his sheep with eternal life ("they shall never perish"). In the Deuteronomy passage, we see no direct statement about the destiny of those who *do* listen to the Prophet, but we see judgment for those who refuse of follow him, "I myself will call him to account." Or, as the Acts 3 text paraphrases the Deuteronomy text, "Anyone who does not listen to him will be completely cut off from among his people.'" As argued above, if unbelief (failure to listen) is correlated with condemnation, perhaps belief is correlated with eternal life.

---

[267] *Tractate Taanith* (Fasting), Chapter 1.
[268] Exodus 32:31-32 with John 12:27

All Who Came Before Me Were Liars

In John 10:8, Yeshua stated, "All who ever came before me were thieves and robbers, but the sheep did not listen to them." The Lord here is not talking about the *First Testament* prophets – for Jesus quoted their words as Scripture – but rather the false Messiahs and false claimants of the Moses-like prophetic title. In Acts 5:35-37, Gamaliel (grandson of Hillel) mentions examples of two such claimants:

> Then he addressed them: "Men of Israel, consider carefully what you intend to do to these men. Some time ago Theudas appeared, claiming to be somebody, and about four hundred men rallied to him. He was killed, all his followers were dispersed, and it all came to nothing. After him, Judas the Galilean appeared in the days of the census and led a band of people in revolt. He too was killed, and all his followers were scattered."

Paying close attention to Gamaliel's words, one phrase stands out, "claiming to be somebody." Whether these self-proclaimed men of God suggested they were the Messiah or the Moses-like Prophet (or both or neither), the text does not specify. By all standards, they were false shepherds.

But the list goes on. Josephus mentions Simon of Perea.[269] Recent finds suggest a pre-Christian tradition that the Messiah would rise again on the third day. Some infer that Simon's followers may have expected a resurrection in his case; yet the connection between the anticipated resurrection of the Messiah and an anticipated resurrection of Simon is far from proven. The pre-Christian idea that the true Messiah would be

---

[269] Flavius Josephus, *Jewish War* 2.57-59 and *Jewish Antiquities* 17.273-277

resurrected on the third day was probably known before Jesus was born, as evidenced by the finding.[270] Luke's Gospel suggests that the *Tanakh* somewhere not only predicts the Messiah would rise again (that is clear in Isaiah 53:11-12), but that he would do so on the third day.[271] The exegesis may not be evident to us, but it seems to have been understood in pre-Christian first century Judaism.

Athrononges was yet another such false Messiah previous to the time of Jesus.[272] We can imagine, based on Jesus' words, that there were many others whose names have been lost to history. The list of men who have claimed to be the Messiah since the time of Jesus is a long one, but that does not eliminate the possibility of another long list before his time!

Summary

Jesus nowhere *stated* that he was the Prophet Moses predicted, but the New Testament does. Yet Yeshua did state that he was greater than the temple,[273] greater than the prophet Jonah,[274] and greater than Solomon.[275] He suggested that he was David's master (Lord),[276] and, by virtue of his pre-existence, greater than Abraham.[277] On the *Mount of*

---

[270] See "Ancient Tablet Ignites Debate on Messiah and Resurrection" by Ethan Bronner is *The New York Times* (online), July 6, 2008, http://www.nytimes.com/2008/07/06/world/middleeast/06stone.html?_r=3&oref=slogin&oref=slogin.
[271] Note Luke 24:46 carefully: "…and He said to them, "Thus it is written, that the Christ would suffer and rise again from the dead the *third* day…"
[272] http://en.wikipedia.org/wiki/Athronges , accessed 4-3-10
[273] Matthew 12:6
[274] Matthew 12:41
[275] Matthew 12:42
[276] Matthew 12:43
[277] John 8:53-54

Transfiguration, both Moses and Elijah minister to Jesus.[278] Yeshua claims that Moses wrote of him;[279] Only Jesus and Jesus alone meets the criteria of the Deuteronomy 18:15-19 passage. He is Lord, Messiah, and the expected Prophet.

---

[278] Matthew 17:3
[279] Luke 24:44

Chapter 9: Midrashim Grace and Faith

(Deut. 8:1-3; 9:4-6 and Luke 14:7-24, Matthew 22:1-14)
(Deuteronomy 7:17-23 with John 14:11-13 and Matthew 17:20, 21:21)

I am a social man who enjoys people. One day, I was chatting with a visitor in our church lobby and he informed me that his daughter's name was Hannah Grace. I suggested that her name was redundant. *Hannah* is the Hebrew word for grace; *Anna* is the Greek version of the name Hannah. *Charis* is the Greek word for grace. We might argue that "grace by any other name is just as gracious!" And it is.

Some Christians do not anticipate finding grace in the *First Testament*; they view grace as strictly a *Second Testament* phenomenon. Although Moses presented the Law and – in contrast – Jesus Christ is said to usher in the era of God's grace,[280] we should not read more into these statements than intended. We should not infer that grace is absent from the Torah, nor should we view Yeshua's ministry of grace as without law.

As a means of justification, grace and law are indeed mutually exclusive; the Law diagnoses our problem, while grace remedies it. The Christian finds strength from God's grace and direction from his law, although the Christian does not relate to God as one "under the Law."[281] The revelation of God's Law is itself an act of grace. It is noteworthy

---

[280] cf. John 1:17; Grace was fully realized through Jesus Christ, but that does not mean it was absent beforehand.
[281] This is one complex subject. To be "under the Law" means to be awaiting the redeemer in a pre-incarnation mode (see Galatians 3:22-29). Yet the Christian life is not without law (demands God makes

that overcoming saints in heaven sing "the song *of Moses* and of the Lamb."[282] Since many modern Christians consider themselves completely disconnected from Moses, the heavenly saints and the earthly saints are out of sync. If we dig deeply into Christ's teachings through *Midrash,* we may find ourselves appreciating Moses' legacy more than we have.

The concept of salvation by grace alone through faith in Christ alone to God's glory alone is a foundational Biblical belief and a distinctive of evangelical doctrine, a viewpoint I support with my entire being. Although the New Testament – and Paul in particular – addresses the concept of grace and faith with great clarity and detail, the ideas of grace and faith did not originate with the Apostle to the Gentiles. *The Second Testament's* instruction about grace, faith, Messiah, and God's glory are rooted in *First Testament* teaching. In this chapter, we will visit the subject of *grace* and note how Yeshua taught about grace via *Midrash.* We will then follow a similar procedure as we examine faith.

Part One: Amazing Grace – Torah Style

The nearest synonym to the word "grace" is "favor."[283] Unlike a wage – which is earned– a favor is *undeserved.* God longs to be favorable toward us, and this favorable disposition is completely unmerited.[284]

---

upon us). Some of these demands were made in the Torah and apply to Israel alone, and thus the entire subject becomes complex. This subject is way beyond the scope of this book.
[282] Revelation 15:3
[283] Lewis Sperry Chafer, *Grace*, pp 3-4.

Although the Scriptures often correlate humility and grace, this correlation is rarely discussed. True humility is an early stage of grace and an evidence of God's gracious working within us.[285]

If it is true that the Lord prepares his own by first humbling them and then showering them with saving grace, then God receives *all* the glory. My understanding of grace is that man is incapable of claiming even a miniscule percentage of credit when it comes to God's gracious work. Grace must be entirely God's doing; if we contribute anything to grace, it is no longer grace.[286]

Man is held responsible for humbling himself. He is responsible to squarely face his spiritual bankruptcy and receive God's grace by faith. The apparent paradox between God's sovereignty and man's responsibility is beyond the scope of this or any book, but we acknowledge it exists.

James quotes from the book of Proverbs to his readers so they will learn that grace correlates with humility: "God opposes the proud but gives grace to the humble."[287]

In our Deuteronomy text, we see a similar pattern: *God humbles the people he intends to bless;* then God pours out grace upon them. As a result, God receives the full glory for

---

[284] Yet grace is correlated to God's just wrath being propitiated and sin expiated. God is gracious in a way that is consistent with his justice. See Romans 5:6-11.

[285] Philippians 2:13 reads, "…for it is God who is at work in you, both to will and to work for His good pleasure."

[286] Romans 11:6 reads, "And if by grace, then it is no longer by works; if it were, grace would no longer be grace." Thus grace and works are mutually exclusive causes, although works can and do issue forth from grace.

[287] James 4:6b; James is quoting Proverbs 3:34.

his acts of grace. To demonstrate this, we will peruse two passages from Deuteronomy, 8:1-3 and 9:4-6.

> 8:1-3: Be careful to follow every command I am giving you today, so that you may live and increase and may enter and possess the land that the LORD promised on oath to your forefathers. Remember how the LORD your God led you all the way in the desert these forty years, to humble you and to test you in order to know what was in your heart, whether or not you would keep his commands. *He humbled you*, causing you to hunger and then feeding you with manna, which neither you nor your fathers had known, to teach you that man does not live on bread alone but on every word that comes from the mouth of the LORD.
>
> 9:4-7 After the LORD your God has driven them out before you, do not say to yourself, "The LORD has brought me here to take possession of this land *because of my righteousness.*" *No*, it is on account of the wickedness of these nations that the LORD is going to drive them out before you. *It is not because of your righteousness or your integrity* that you are going in to take possession of their land; but on account of the wickedness of these nations, the LORD your God will drive them out before you, to accomplish what he swore to your fathers, to Abraham, Isaac and Jacob. *Understand, then, that it is not because of your righteousness that the LORD your God is giving you this good land to possess, for you are a stiff-necked people.*

We spent some time examining Deuteronomy 8 in Chapter Four, contemplating its implications about wealth. I am proposing that Yeshua derived other *Midrashim* from this same rich text. So we will re-examine Deuteronomy 8 from the angle of grace, while adding the Deuteronomy 9 grace passage into the mix.

➢ *God's Grace to the Hebrews*

Yahweh exalts those who do not merit his blessing. He does not exalt all the unworthy, but those he chooses to exalt. Many nations were resistant to God, and Israel was certainly one of them. The text describes them as a "stiff-necked," stubborn people – a compliment in no culture. God says in no uncertain terms that *his blessings were not correlated to their righteousness*.

Later Jews did not always have the correct perspective about God's grace. Some spoke of "meriting" a place in the world to come. Here is just one *Talmud* portion demonstrating this idea: "…if others will enter [the future world] in their merit, surely they themselves most certainly will!"[288]

God loves to turn the tables by exalting those who have no personal claim to his goodness. Deuteronomy 9:6 reads, "… *it is not because of your righteousness* that the LORD your God is giving you this good land to possess…" The Exodus Hebrews, who made up the original Exodus generation, were a motley crew with a victim mentality. They were a nation of slaves, whose special expertise included fickleness, complaining, doubting, and whining. This was the nation God chose to bless, and God's choice was an irrevocable one.[289]

> *Not Everyone Experiences God's Grace to the Same Extent*

The Scriptures assert that God extends his grace to the humble and repentant. Yet Yahweh harshly judges those who refuse to repent, as cited in Deuteronomy 9:4-7. On the one hand, God freely gives the rich land of Canaan to the Hebrews, but, on the other

---

[288] *Sanhedrin 110b*

[289] Romans 11:28-29, "As far as the gospel is concerned, they are enemies on your account; but as far as election is concerned, they are loved on account of the patriarchs, for God's gifts and his call are irrevocable." God could delay bringing the Hebrews into Canaan, but he could not desert them forever.

hand, he does so at the expense of Canaanite lives and property. Looking at matters theologically, Yahweh took land from the *non-repentant* Canaanites and graciously gave that land to the *undeserving* Jews.

God treats all fairly, but his fairness is not correlated with *equal* treatment. Thus God is just to mandate the genocide of a morally and spiritually depraved people, yet he is free to give their territory to others who are undeserving. Fairness wrongs no one and treats no one more harshly than justice demands, but grace – undeserved favor extending beyond justice – may be given or withheld.[290] His grace goes beyond justice, but not contrary to it. God has the prerogative of being as gracious as he pleases.[291] Thus we covet God's grace in our lives, not his justice. In truth, all experience some level of God's grace,[292] but some of us are lavished with it.[293]

To clear his name from the accusation of injustice, God walked the extra mile by patiently waiting, giving time for the unrighteous Canaanites (Amorites) to repent. About 400 years before the Exodus, God set the judgment timer and revealed the time framework to Abraham. We read in Genesis 15:16:

---

[290] In Jesus' parable of the Vineyard (Matthew 20:1-16) verse 15 summarizes the right of the owner, "Don't I have the right to do what I want with my own money? Or are you envious because I am generous?" God is free to be as generous as he pleases, as long as no one is cheated in the process.

[291] Psalm 115:3 (NASB): "But our God is in the heavens; He does whatever He pleases."

[292] For a fine discussion on the subject of "Common Grace," see Wayne Grudem, *Systematic Theology*, pp. 657-668.

[293] Ephesians 1:7-9 is written to believers: "In him we have redemption through his blood, the forgiveness of sins, in accordance with *the riches of God's grace that he lavished on us* with all wisdom and understanding. And he made known to us the mystery of his will according to his good pleasure, which he purposed in Christ…"

> In the fourth generation your descendants will come back here, for the sin of the Amorites has not yet reached its full measure.

Since the new generation of Hebrews recognized their status as the "least of all people," they were postured to experience God's grace. They knew that their fathers did not deserve to be delivered from Egypt, they knew they did not deserve to be given the land of Canaan, and they knew they could only conquer the land with God's help. Centuries later, because the Jewish people did not humbly embrace their Messiah, Israel was disciplined through the destruction of Jerusalem and her dispersion throughout the world. This dispersion lasted nearly 1900 years. God promises he will one day visit Israel with salvation when he humbles them and they receive their pierced Messiah.[294]

Jesus Midrash on Grace and Humility

I believe Jesus may have had these Deuteronomy verses in mind when he observed table guests posturing for the most prestigious seats at the table. A number of parables mentioned below could be connected to his *Midrash* on these texts.

The Gospel writers would want to capture what was unique in Yeshua's teaching, not repeat teachings that could also be had from other rabbis or the Torah itself. The Deuteronomy verses were never far from Yeshua's mind, nor those of his audience. The

---

[294] This is too broad a subject to address here, but some relevant Scriptures to peruse include: Zechariah 12-14, esp. 12:8-10, Jeremiah 31:35-37, Romans 11:25-32.

entire nation was absorbed with learning the meaning of the Torah, and Deuteronomy in particular.[295]

Luke 14:7-14, quoted below, taps into the Deuteronomy verses regarding humility. Here, we are proactively taught to pursue humility. Once again, the emphasis is on the individual and demands a proactive approach.

> When he noticed how the guests picked the places of honor at the table, he told them this parable: "When someone invites you to a wedding feast, do not take the place of honor, for a person more distinguished than you may have been invited. If so, the host who invited both of you will come and say to you, 'Give this man your seat.' Then, humiliated, you will have to take the least important place. But when you are invited, take the lowest place, so that when your host comes, he will say to you, 'Friend, move up to a better place.' Then you will be honored in the presence of all your fellow guests. For everyone who exalts himself will be humbled, and he who humbles himself will be exalted."
>
> Then Jesus said to his host, "When you give a luncheon or dinner, do not invite your friends, your brothers or relatives, or your rich neighbors; if you do, they may invite you back and so you will be repaid. But when you give a banquet, invite the poor, the crippled, the lame, the blind, and you will be blessed. Although they cannot repay you, you will be repaid at the resurrection of the righteous."

---

[295] Dr. Jeffrey Tigay, in an article titled, "Deuteronomy," writes, "Deuteronomy strongly influenced later Jewish tradition. The core of Jewish worship is the recitation of the *Shema* (6:4) and the public reading of the Torah (rooted in 31: 11). Also based on Deuteronomy are the duty of blessing God after meals (*Birkat haMazon*, 8: 10), *Kiddush* [a prayer of sanctification] on *Shabbat* (5:12), affixing *mezuzot* to doorposts, wearing *tefillin* (phylacteries) (6:8 9, 11:18, 20) and *tzitzit* (tassels) (22:12), and charity to the poor (e.g., 15:8).

Deuteronomy is the source of the concept that religious life should be based on a sacred book and its study. As the biblical book that deals most explicitly with beliefs and attitudes, it plays a major role in Jewish theology. In the theological ethical introduction of his digest of Jewish law, the *Mishnah Torah*, Maimonides cites Deuteronomy more than any other book, starting with the command to believe in God and Him alone.

Deuteronomy's effect on Jewish life cannot be overstated. No idea has shaped Jewish history more than monotheism, which this book asserts so passionately" [source: www.myjewishlearning.com/texts/Bible/Torah/Deuteronomy.shtml, accessed 5-8-10].

> *Since God Values Humility, We Should Humble Ourselves*

Jesus' axiom about humility rings clear and true: "For everyone who exalts himself will be humbled, and he who humbles himself will be exalted." When Jerusalem was under siege by the Babylonians, Ezekiel (21:26) prophesied God's judgment upon his people:

> …this is what the Sovereign LORD says: Take off the turban, remove the crown. It will not be as it was: The lowly will be exalted and the exalted will be brought low…

In Moses day, the Hebrews were arrogant on an individual basis. The same might be said of the Jews during the days of Ezekiel. Yahweh is not merely concerned about the collective; he is also Lord of the individual. And what is the collective, but the accumulation of individuals?

The *Talmud* contains a statement similar to Jesus' and Ezekiel's truism:

> He who humbles himself, him will God elevate; he who elevates himself, him will God humiliate. He who runs after greatness, from him greatness will flee; he who flees from greatness, him will greatness follow.[296]

Hillel said:

> Remove from thy place two or three rows of seats and wait until they call thee back.[297]

We can conclude that Yeshua's teaching about humility was consistent with that of other rabbis, particularly *Bet Hillel*.

---

[296] *'Er. 13a* cited in *The Jewish Encyclopedia*, "Humility," www.jewishencyclopedia.com, accessed 4-28-10.
[297] *Lev. R. i.,* cited in *The Jewish Encyclopedia* as per above.

In Messiah's first illustration, we are exhorted to avoid exalting ourselves by seeking prestige and recognition. In his second teaching, we are told to *intentionally* associate with the humble and downtrodden. Humility is proactive and often counter-intuitive. Isaiah 61:1-2 reflects a similar tone:

> This is what the LORD says: "Heaven is my throne, and the earth is my footstool. Where is the house you will build for me? Where will my resting place be? Has not my hand made all these things, and so they came into being?" declares the LORD. "This is the one I esteem: he who is humble and contrite in spirit, and trembles at my word."

Yeshua's *Midrash* about humility may have been additionally influenced by verses like this passage in Isaiah and the above cited Ezekiel 21:26.

➢ *Yahweh embraces the humble*

Jesus taught another parable found in Matthew 22:1-14, called *The Parable of the Banquet*. The idea of this story is that these guests had been *previously* invited and had already indicated that they would be attending the banquet. When the banquet was prepared and ready, these guests defaulted on their commitment. They made excuses to justify their fickleness; their excuses were shallow; their arrogant indifference was obvious.

The master instructed his servants to haul in whomever they could find, whether good and bad, rich or poor. Those willing to attend were recipients of the hosts' grace. One, however, did not bother to change into proper attire; he was cast out while the others feasted. The parable's lesson seems to be twofold: (1) the unworthy who respond enjoy great blessing while non-responsive peers have no idea what they missed, and (2) those who seek to avail themselves of grace but hang on to their contemptuous attitude will not enjoy what they anticipated. Even though one is offered a blessing by grace, viewing the host with contempt reveals an unreceptive heart controlled by *incognito* arrogance.

The *Talmud* records a similar parable by Rabbi Johanan b. Zakkai:

> [It is like] a king who invited his servants to a feast and did not appoint them a time. The wise among them adorned themselves and sat down by the door of the palace, for they said: Is anything lacking in a palace? The foolish among them went to their work, for they said: Is a feast ever given without preparation? Suddenly the king summoned his servants. The wise among them went in before him adorned as they were, and the foolish went in before him in their working clothes. The king rejoiced to see the wise and was angry to see the foolish, and said: These who adorned themselves for the feast shall sit down and eat and drink; but those who did not adorn themselves for the feast shall stand and look on.[298]

> ➤ *Grace is reserved for those who will receive it humbly*

God's graciousness does not excuse those who reject him. Just as the Canaanites were removed from Canaan to make room for the Israelites, so those who reject the Lord's invitation are cleared out for those (sometimes unlikely) people who respond. We might find within Yeshua's parable the concept that his original audience – comprising mostly Jews – would mostly reject his message, while his "other sheep" (gentiles) would embrace it – and thus feast eternally at God's banquet table. Isaiah 25:6-

---

[298] *b. Shabbat 153a*, cited by www.crossmarks.com/parable/5supper.htm in an article titled, "Just Don't Call Me Late for Supper: The Parable of the Great Supper" accessed 4-29-10.

9 seems to support the idea that people from all nations will be included in the glorious future banquet:

> "On this mountain the LORD Almighty will prepare a feast of rich food for all peoples, a banquet of aged wine— the best of meats and the finest of wines. On this mountain he will destroy the shroud that enfolds all peoples, the sheet that covers all nations; he will swallow up death forever. The Sovereign LORD will wipe away the tears from all faces; he will remove the disgrace of his people from all the earth. The LORD has spoken. In that day they will say, 'Surely this is our God; we trusted in him, and he saved us. This is the LORD, we trusted in him; let us rejoice and be glad in his salvation.'"

The Parable of the Pharisee and the Tax Collector is another indication that receiving grace is correlated to humility. In Luke 18:9-17, Jesus taught that the devoutly religious self-righteous Pharisee left the temple without being forgiven because he was among those who "…trusted in themselves that they were righteous, and viewed others with contempt" (9b). The tax collector, on the other hand, having no sense of self-righteous, asked God for mercy.[299] The tax collector left justified (righteous) in God's eyes, not the Pharisee. Once again we see the correlation between genuine humility and God's grace. Humility is simply adjusting to reality; we learn to accept that God is holy and we are not, and thus we reverence him (unlike the fellow who showed up to the banquet without the proper attire). We acknowledge the limitation of human nature and our own personal limitations. We realize we are completely depraved, meaning *we have nothing*

---

[299] We may think of grace as God giving us blessings we do not deserve, and mercy as God withholding his wrath or judgment we do deserve. Thus they are joined together in I Timothy 1:2, 2 Timothy 1:2, Hebrews 4:16 and 2 John 1:3.

meritorious to offer God. We accept the reality of our own vulnerability and the bleak reality that our hearts are deceitful and desperately wicked. Our righteous deeds are like filthy rags,[300] and we can only approach God through the blood sacrifice of Jesus Christ shed on the cross two millennia ago. It is when we find ourselves completely hopeless about our ability to please God – or offer brownie points – that we become truly open to receive God's grace.

Arrogance lures many to numerous alternatives, one that preserves our pride and allows us to partly help ourselves. But until we see ourselves in need of a savior who saves *completely*, we are unlikely to <u>fully</u> embrace Yeshua as our Redeemer.

Dr. Stuart Sacks discusses the failure of modern mainstream Judaism to move beyond sin-management to find God's grace in the new birth. This is sadly true with many who profess some form of Christianity as well.

> A weakness of conventional Judaism has been its attention to sins rather than to man's fallenness. Because the heart is hopelessly diseased, a radical cure must be found if man's relationship with God is to be healed, if man is to approach God with confidence…the tax collector has asked for mercy…. He returns home "justified," "righteous," "acquitted of his sins." By grace, he has been "exalted."[301]

Humility – not substitutes like harsh treatment of the body[302] or putting oneself down – should be a conscious pursuit. We need to take the advice of Yeshua to associate with the

---

[300] cf. Isaiah 64:6
[301] Dr. Stuart Sacks, *Hebrews Through A Hebrews Eyes*, pp. 39-40.
[302] Colossians 2:23 is regularly ignored in some circles, "Such regulations indeed have an appearance of wisdom, with their self-imposed worship, their false humility and their harsh treatment of the body, but

lowly and be ever conscious of the reality of our failings. Yet inflating our sinfulness is nothing more than sanctified lying.

Part Two: Faith Can Move Mountains – Sometimes a Spoonful at a Time!

Faith is taking God at his Word. Hebrews instructs us, "Now faith is being sure of what we hope for and certain of what we do not see." Whereas wisdom generally says, "A bird in the hand is worth two in the bush," faith says, "If God has spoken, we'll take the two in the bush."

> ➢ *Why is faith so important?*

The Scriptures assert salvation by grace through faith (Romans 5:1, Ephesians 2:8-8). But why is faith the subjective vehicle through which we receive the objective work of Jesus' gracious atonement? And why is faith such a crucial virtue in the Christian life?

The answer, I believe, is this: Faith glorifies God because it demonstrates that the one exercising it considers God's character trustworthy! Doubt insults God, because to doubt means to call Yahweh's character into question.

Faith – in its purest sense – is based upon a clear word from the Lord. To be unsure of God's will because the Scriptures do not address a matter is understandable; to doubt what he has clearly revealed, however, is to insult his integrity.

---

they lack any value in restraining sensual indulgence." Stricter is not always better. Remember, Jesus did not make the grade of the School of Shammai and was condemned for it. See Matthew 9:14-15 and 11:16-19.

Although we may exercise faith about a matter in which we sense God's leading, we must confess that we might be and sometimes are wrong in discerning his will. Being "led by the Spirit" is far from an exact science. Our certainty must be directed toward what God can do, particularly when we have no sure word about what he plans to do. In contrast, when Yeshua spoke, his disciples had a clear and definitive word.

Although the *Second Testament* develops the theme of faith, many New Testament teachings could be *Midrashim* waiting to be discovered.

> *Faith: Little by Little*

The Exodus generation was strapped by fear and unbelief, so they failed to enter the land "flowing with milk and honey." The Book of Hebrews includes extended *Midrashim* about this subject, including the controversial Hebrews 6 chapter."[303] It is not only Jesus who teaches *Midrash* from the *Tanakh*.

In the text quoted below, God promises the new generation that they and their heirs would conquer Canaan in gradual stages. The task was formidable. This new, current generation of Hebrews would but begin the conquest without seeing its final result; the rewards of faith would accumulate and be realized generations later.

---

[303] Hebrews 6:1-8 is an obvious Midrash from Numbers 13-14; the people saw the produce and tasted of what potentially awaited them in the future (13:27); yet, they were conquered by unbelief; after determining not to enter Canaan, the Hebrews later changed their minds, but it was too late (Numbers 14:39-45). Hebrews 2-3 are also clearly based on the events of Numbers 13-14.

I believe a number of Yeshua's *Midrashim* about faith find their source in Deuteronomy 7:17-23:

> You may say to yourselves, "These nations are stronger than we are. How can we drive them out?" But do not be afraid of them; remember well what the LORD your God did to Pharaoh and to all Egypt. You saw with your own eyes the great trials, the miraculous signs and wonders, the mighty hand and outstretched arm, with which the LORD your God brought you out. The LORD your God will do the same to all the peoples you now fear. Moreover, the LORD your God will send the hornet among them until even the survivors who hide from you have perished. Do not be terrified by them, for the LORD your God, who is among you, is a great and awesome God. The LORD your God will drive out those nations before you, little by little. You will not be allowed to eliminate them all at once, or the wild animals will multiply around you. But the LORD your God will deliver them over to you, throwing them into great confusion until they are destroyed.

John 14:11-13, a problematic text, makes more sense if we postulate that it, too, is a *Midrash* on the Deuteronomy text above:

> Believe me when I say that I am in the Father and the Father is in me; or at least believe on the evidence of the miracles themselves. I tell you the truth, anyone who has faith in me will do what I have been doing. He will do even greater things than these, because I am going to the Father. And I will do whatever you ask in my name, so that the Son may bring glory to the Father.

These verses seem puzzling; even the great miracle-working apostles like Peter, Paul, and John did not match the miraculous workings of Jesus. Could Yeshua be referring to the collective, long-term accomplishments of his church over the years when he says, "He will do even greater things than these…?"

> ➢ *Our Man Joshua and Greater Things*

Let us turn our attention to the man who helped initiate the promised conquest of Canaan: Joshua. If you think about it, Joshua actually did more to conquer the Promised Land than did his prestigious mentor, Moses. Although Moses' ministry paved the way for Joshua, Joshua was the man who actually engaged the military.

In a similar sense, Yeshua provided for our salvation. All the events of history are in the background when compared to Jesus' atoning death, burial, resurrection, and ascension. Yet, when it comes to actually building up the church body *and spreading the news* of the Kingdom, Christians have a ministry so unique that even Jesus' ministry did not parallel it! In one sense, Jesus accomplished the victory, but we spread the victory around! Thus, in one sense, fulfilling the Great Commission of Matthew 28 is perhaps the "greater work."

Unlike miraculous healings that were quick and to the point, Yeshua's disciples are to administer the slow, gradual conquests of faith.

> *How far did Joshua get?*

When it came to conquering Canaan, the Deuteronomy text implies that a gradual victory meant a solid victory. But let's note what actually happened in Israel's history, as Kenneth A Kitchen summarizes:

> …The Book of Joshua does not describe a total Hebrew conquest and occupation of Canaan, real or imaginary. Read straight, its narratives describe an entry (from over the Jordan), full destruction of two minor centers (Jericho, Ai; burned), then defeat of local kings and raids through south Canaan. Towns are attacked, taken and damaged ("destroyed"), kings and subjects killed and then left behind, not held on to. The

same in north Canaan: strategic Hazor is fully destroyed (burned), but no others. The rest are treated like the southern towns, and again left, not held. Israel stayed based in Gilgal, then took over an inland strip from there up to Shechem and Tirzah. These preliminary successes were celebrated with war rhetoric appropriate to the time, which should not be twisted to mean what it does not. Joshua made allocations not taken up while he yet lived…[304]

Thus the conquest of Canaan took 400 years. Not until the latter life of David was the conquest complete. We can see here that the fruit of faith can be directed toward generations centuries away.

We might suggest that Yeshua corresponds in analogy to Moses, and we individual believers correspond to Joshua's army. In another sense, however, Joshua might be a type of Jesus. Joshua parceled out the land and broke the stronghold of Canaan's powerful kings, but the people were responsible to conquer their assigned allotments.

In the church, Jesus has defeated Satan while the Kingdom of God is breaking forth in us and through us. We are not conquering a physical land, but we are seeking to reach people from every tribe, kindred and nation and thus build his Kingdom. The commanding statement Yeshua made in Acts 1:8 (KJV) describes our task, one accomplished over time via faith:

> "But ye shall receive power, after that the Holy Ghost is come upon you: and ye shall be witnesses unto me both in Jerusalem, and in all Judaea, and in Samaria, and unto the uttermost part of the earth."

> ➢ *Faith: A Little Can Accomplish the Impossible*

---

[304] Kenneth A. Kitchen, *On the Reliability of the Old Testament*, pp. 234-235.

In the Deuteronomy 7:17-23 passage cited above, faith neutralizes fear. The Hebrews were told not to fear the seemingly impossible because God is not limited by statistics. Yeshua adds to the discussion in Matthew 17:20:

> "… I tell you the truth, if you have faith as small as a mustard seed, you can say to this mountain, 'Move from here to there' and it will move. Nothing will be impossible for you."

He adds even more while teaching about faith in Matthew 21:21-22; the setting is the shriveled and cursed fig tree.

> Jesus replied, "I tell you the truth, if you have faith and do not doubt, not only can you do what was done to the fig tree, but also you can say to this mountain, 'Go, throw yourself into the sea,' and it will be done. If you believe, you will receive whatever you ask for in prayer."

We may distill the principle to this: God uses our faith to accomplish what seems impossible. This simple statement packs a powerful punch.

Yeshua was not the only Jewish voice to publicize this idea. Rabbi Eliezer the Great phrased it this way:

> Whoever has a piece of bread in his basket and says, "What shall I eat tomorrow?" belongs only to them who are little in faith. [305]

➢ *Faith as a mustard seed*

The mustard seed is the smallest seed that farmers sowed. The tiny size of the mustard seed – and the large plant it produces – illustrates two ideas: (1) a little faith goes a long

---

[305] *Sotah 48b*

way, and (2) potent faith might be reserved and subtle. Perhaps this second idea explains why Yeshua commanded his followers to do their works of righteousness discreetly, not to be seen by men. In the *Talmud,* we note an interesting comment that also suggests strong faith is discreet:

> "'One who says the *Tefillah* so that it can be heard is of the small of faith; he who raises his voice in praying is of the false prophets; he who belches and yawns is of the arrogant; if he sneezes during his prayer it is a bad sign for him — some say, it shows that he is a low fellow; one who spits during his prayer is like one who spits before a king'."[306]

The kind of "mustard seed" faith Jesus advocates can make a big difference in life or the kingdom, but nurtures neither pride nor boasting. Yeshua illustrates the power of this faith through two illustrations, the latter *hyperbole*. The first is that of the fig tree. The fact that the tree had shriveled up after Christ's curse is a miracle, but more than a miracle. It presaged Yahweh's judgment upon Israel for rejecting their Messiah. The fig tree will blossom in the end times, when Israel prepares to receive her Messiah.[307]

In some ways, Yeshua's two illustrations are not compatible. Jesus actually cursed a fig tree and it actually wilted, so this illustration is based upon a historical happening. The other illustration – telling a mountain to move and plunk into the sea – has never happened to date, and thus hypothetical. Despite the incompatibility, the overall lesson is clear: faith can accomplish the impossible. Other passages add nuances to this concept.

---

[306] *Berakoth 24b*
[307] Matthew 24:32-33, 23:39

For example, faith is correlated with prayer and only effective when it is "according to God's will."[308] We cannot generate faith by clenching our teeth and creating a determined attitude, but faith is a gift finding its source in God.[309] Our faith grows stronger as we bury ourselves in the Word of God.[310] Unfortunately, we do not always embrace the faith he gives us.

On the other hand, if we do not exercise faith and pray, then we may not fulfill God's desired will for us. God's determined will cannot be resisted, his desired will is conditioned upon man's response – and therefore not always accomplished.[311] James harmonizes matters by declaring, "You do not have, because you do not ask God."[312] Faith cannot appropriate that which is outside of God's will, but some things that are within God's can only be appropriated by faith; these may remain unclaimed if not prayerfully requested through faith.

Chapter Summary

---

[308] I John 5:14

[309] In I Corinthians 12:9, we see an overall spiritual gift of faith but gifts (instances) of healing: "…to another faith by the same Spirit, to another gifts of healing by that one Spirit…" Miraculous instances may not be the result of a resident spiritual gift, but may be given by God for a particular instance; thus the Lord may give us an unusual instance of faith to accomplish something for his purposes.

[310] See Romans 10:17.

[311] Two Greek words are translated as God's *will* in the New Testament: *boulemai* and *thelo*. Colin Brown asserts that at the time of the New Testament, the words were used fairly interchangeably (see Colin Brown, *The New International Dictionary of New Testament Theology*, Volume 3, pp. 1015-1023). From a theological, interpretive perspective, however, two "tracks" regarding God's will seem clear: his providential, decreed will and the revelation of what he demands of us. See Wayne Grudem, *Systematic Theology*, pp. 315-354 for an enlightening discussion of this subject.

[312] James 4:2b.

When we increase context by locating the texts Yeshua uses for his *Midrashim* about grace and faith, we correct modern abuses of these concepts and embrace fuller perspectives. Biblical faith, for example, does not eliminate hardships or heartaches from life. Biblical faith may stretch and stress us, but faith is not primarily about us. Biblical faith exalts God, builds his kingdom, and helps us to live in ways that please him.

Like Joshua and the conquest, faith is a long-term proposition!

Faith is only effective because of God's grace, for it appropriates what God has graciously offered. When we have humbled ourselves and have lost all confidence "in the flesh," then we find it natural to reach out to the only one who can provide, our gracious God! This is true of salvation, but is also true of the entire Christian life, a life that begins with faith and continues on by faith.[313]

---

[313] See Galatians 3:1-14.

Chapter 10: Discipleship Midrash

(I Kings 19:1-21 with Mathew 4:1-11, Luke 9:57-62, Matthew 19:21, Luke 5:27)

Discipleship is a controversial subject. In the evangelical Christian world, some have suggested that one can be saved (regenerate and heaven-bound) by faith in Christ without becoming one of his disciples. Others propose the opposite extreme: one cannot be saved without completely surrendering his or her life to Jesus Christ.[314] Such debates frequently detach themselves from the realities of what it meant to be a disciple within first century Judaism. The definition of the word "disciple" has become more specific than its Biblical (and Jewish) usage. From a theological viewpoint, we might argue that the term "disciple" is actually a broader term than "believer"[315] and not the other way around.[316] While debating, some inflate the commitment level of the early church.[317] In addition,

---

[314] *The Gospel According to Jesus* by John F. MacArthur is perhaps the premiere work advocating "Lordship Salvation."

[315] John 6:66 makes the point: "After this many of his disciples turned back and no longer walked with him…"

[316] In Mark 5:18-20, a formerly demonized man asks to follow Yeshua (we can read "as a disciple" into the text), but Jesus tells him otherwise: "As Jesus was getting into the boat, the man who had been demon-possessed begged to go with him. Jesus did not let him, but said, 'Go home to your family and tell them how much the Lord has done for you, and how he has had mercy on you.' So the man went away and began to tell in the Decapolis how much Jesus had done for him. And all the people were amazed."
Jesus healed many people who did not follow him in discipleship but yet believed and were transformed, In contrast, many who followed him as disciples later turned away from him.
These insights have been apparent for centuries, yet often ignored; this demonstrates how dangerous it is when we form a "science" around "what preaches." Most "discipleship materials" rarely examine these fundamental assumptions about discipleship.

[317] Although we tend to focus upon the heroes within the first century church, we would do well to pay attention to the implications of some of Paul's statements. Take, for example, Philippians 2:19-21 (ESV), "I hope in the Lord Jesus to send Timothy to you soon, so that I too may be cheered by news of you. For I

many of Yeshua's specific demands are wrongly interpreted as prescriptive principles applying to all situations and to all his followers in all circumstances. If we stir another factor into the caldron of confusion – namely the *temporary* nature of the disciple's hardships[318] we can understand why the subject of discipleship leaves so many Christians actually groping, trying to harmonize what is not meant to be harmonized, completely unaware of how blind most of us are in these areas.

Some facts are actually simple: believers were called disciples long before they were ever called Christians.[319] In addition, we see distinctions within the Gospels between what Yeshua demanded of differing individuals.[320] "Discipleship" is not an exact science with consistent formulas, as it is made out to be.

---

have no one like him, who will be genuinely concerned for your welfare. For they **all** seek their own interests, not those of Jesus Christ."

It seems obvious that the early believers struggled with consistent surrender as do we modern believers. Although Paul's team workers were considered the cream of the crop, note his words of disappointment in 2 Timothy 4:16-17, "At my first defense no one came to stand by me, but all deserted me. May it not be charged against them! But the Lord stood by me and strengthened me, so that through me the message might be fully proclaimed and all the Gentiles might hear it. So I was rescued from the lion's mouth." The problem with the "complete surrender" theory is that assurance of salvation would not be possible; one cannot be sure he is completely surrendered in all areas until he is tested in all areas. A middle ground of repentance and faith with a desire to follow Christ seems to best describe saving faith (see Acts 20:21). It was the serious attempt to learn and implement the rabbi's teaching that made one a true disciple, but disciples still had their struggles and areas of resistance.

[318] Although the idea of "counting the cost" is applicable to modern disciples, the nature of discipleship is the same only in *principle*, not particulars. Yeshua does not call most of us to leave spouses and children and roam around with a spiritual leader for a few months. With the gospel spreading outside of the Jewish culture, a steadier form of discipleship has replaced the old Jewish one – a consistent determination to "grow in the grace and knowledge of our Lord Jesus Christ" (2 Peter 3:18).

[319] Acts 11:26b (KJV) states, "And the disciples were called Christians first in Antioch."

[320] In Matthew 19:21, Yeshua demands a potential disciple sell all that he has (on hand); in Luke 19:8, Christ is pleased that Zacchaeus donated *half* of his possessions to the poor. In Luke 5:27, Yeshua tells Levi (Matthew) to leave his work and "follow me." In Mark 5:18-20, the formerly demon-possessed man

If we are going to talk about Jesus' disciples, we have to begin with the Master Rabbi, Yeshua himself. From the human perspective, how was Yeshua *postured* as a rabbi? What was his relationship to the Oral Law being espoused by some of his contemporaries, for example? Where did he stand among his contemporaries? We examined this theme briefly in chapter one, but we need to expand our thinking further.

Jesus Favored *Bet Hillel* But That Does Not Mean He Was A Pharisee

Yeshua often agreed with the Pharisees, but this does not mean he considered himself a Pharisee. Although Christ was caught in the crossfire between the Pharisees from *Bet Shammai* and the Pharisees from *Bet Hillel*, we have no reason to believe that Yeshua would have identified himself as any category of Pharisee.[321]

The New Testament authors – and apparently Jesus himself – referred to the "Pharisees" as though a single group. Yeshua *may* have originally used qualifiers that were not preserved in the Gospels. For example, Christ may have said, "The Pharisees of *Bet Shammai*…" Perhaps the memorized, transmitted version may have omitted the "*Bet Shammai*" qualifiers. But who really knows? This is pure conjecture. What we can say is this: the Holy Spirit inspired the Gospel authors to paint with a broad brush when it came to the Pharisees – and the Jews in general. Why this is so remains an open question.

---

wanted to follow Jesus, but Christ refused his offer and told the man to bear testimony to his family and friends.

[321] Harvey Falk, even in the title of his book, *Jesus the Pharisee*, implies otherwise. Falk has overstated the case, in my opinion.

As a rabbi (sage), Yeshua probably would have categorized himself as an "independent." *Bet Hillel* would have been comfortable with Yeshua's rulings and thus more favorable toward him in contrast to *Bet Shammai*. Still, we need to remind ourselves of this fact: Saul of Tarsus (Paul), the persecutor of the church, was trained by Hillel's grandson, Gamaliel. If Yeshua were a Pharisee identified with *Bet Hillel*, it would seem odd that Saul would so aggressively persecute Yeshua's followers!

Bet Hillel had not earned a reputation for persecution or harshness – as did *Bet Shammai*. Messianic Judaism (Christianity) must have been perceived as so heretical and such a deviant form of Judaism that Saul of Tarsus felt justified breaking with *Bet Hillel's* peaceful legacy. Saul's collaboration with the High Priest (a Sadducee) and the leaders of *Bet Shammai* would have been an unpleasant alliance. Thus Saul and his newfound allies shared a common fear that Messianic Judaism would prevail. Even theological war makes for strange bed fellows. Paul explains his alliance in Acts 22:4-6 (ESV):

> "I am a Jew, born in Tarsus in Cilicia, but brought up in this city, educated at the feet of Gamaliel according to the strict manner of the law of our fathers, being zealous for God as all of you are this day. I persecuted this Way to the death, binding and delivering to prison both men and women, as the high priest and the whole council of elders can bear me witness. From them I received letters to the brothers, and I journeyed toward Damascus to take those also who were there and bring them in bonds to Jerusalem to be punished."

Interestingly, Saul's determination to persecute Christians contradicted the direction established by his immediate teacher, Gamaliel. As you recall, Gamaliel spoke out *against* persecuting the apostles in Acts 5:33-40. Although it is possible that Gamaliel had swallowed his pride and changed his mind, I think this unlikely. After all, Gamaliel's comments were made before the Sanhedrin and convinced the council not to persecute the church.

Yeshua and the Oral Law

A disciple was not allowed to commit his rabbi's teachings to writing. Instead, he would spend most of his time memorizing and reciting the sage's teachings to other disciples.[322] I have already suggested how such patterns of memorization make the "Q Document" theory unnecessary: the teachings and miracles of Yeshua would have been committed to memory by all his followers.

Much of the memorized teaching of the early rabbis was considered the "Oral Law" passed down by Moses – even though it was spoken by rabbis who lived centuries after Moses. Michael L. Brown summarizes the Orthodox Jewish belief: "....Moses not only received the entire Hebrew Bible on Mount Sinai, he received the entire Mishnah and *Talmud*..."[323]

We might think it absurd that Moses received the help of rabbis who lived more than 1500 years later than he did, but this is what such a belief dictates. During the time of Jesus, however, it is not a given that all or even most Jews viewed the teachings of the sages as on par with the written Torah. Even in modern times, Karaite Jews believe in

---

[322] *Ibid*, pp.33-36.
[323] Michael L. Brown, *Answering Jewish Objections to Jesus, Volume Five*, p. 21.

the entire *First Testament* (the *Tanakh*) while rejecting the *Talmud* (Oral Law) as authoritative.[324] In a sense, Karaites are the Jewish equivalent of "Sola Scriptura" evangelicals, like this author.

Nehemia Gordon, himself a Karaite, suggests that Yeshua embraced the Karaite viewpoint regarding the Scriptures, rejecting "the traditions of men"[325] as authoritative. I think Gordon's point is well taken.[326]

Jacob Neusner suggests that the Oral Law (*Mishnah*, the earliest section of the *Talmud*) was considered more authoritative *after* it was written down:

> I refer to the Mishnah, a philosophical law code that reached closure about 200 C.E. and soon afterward was represented as part of the Torah God had revealed to Moses at Sinai. This component of the Torah represented revelation that was orally formulated and orally transmitted. The advent of the Mishnah in circa 200 demanded that people explain the status and authority of the new document. The Mishnah rapidly was accorded the status of the authoritative law-code of Judaism…[327]

Thus we can suggest that the Jewish perspective about the authoritarian nature of the Oral Law was in the process of formulation in the early first century. I suspect that Yeshua's viewpoint regarding the Oral Law is similar to that of Dr. Louis Goldberg:

> First, as already noted from Hillel's and Ishmael's rules of hermeneutics, a good part of the Oral Law reflects sound interpretations of the Written Law and can be used appropriately on many occasions when seeking to enhance the witness of Messianic Jews.

---

[324] Nehemia Gordon, *The Hebrew Yeshua Vs. The Greek Jesus*, pp. 55-56; see also pp. 15-22.
[325] *Ibid.*, pp. 23-27.
[326] In Mark 7:9, Yeshua seems to echo modern Karaite belief, "And he said to them: 'You have a fine way of setting aside the commands of God in order to observe your own traditions!" (NASB).
[327] Jacob Neusner, *A Midrash Reader*, p. 9.

Second, some features of the Oral Law can be adapted by believers to express a scriptural faith.

And third, certain elements of the Oral Law go far beyond and are even contrary to the Written Law.[328]

Since the *Talmud* did not even begin to be written down until the second century[329] (while memorized sayings date back to 200 B.C.), and since the Gospels were penned in the first century, this leads us to a conclusion: The early Messianic believers did not consider Jesus' teachings mere Oral Torah or typical Rabbinic teaching. No, it seems they viewed Yeshua's teachings as truly unique and elevated. Thus the Messianic Community attached a special authority to the written Gospels from the start. I would suggest that if they were not immediately viewed as Scripture, they were viewed as equal or superior to the *Tanakh* in relevance and authority.

Discipleship for Dummies

> *Basics of Discipleship Reviewed*

By way or review and expansion of material covered in chapter one, Jesus was one of hundreds of first century rabbis who roamed the countryside with his respective band of disciples. The Jewish people were socially conditioned to offer hospitality toward traveling rabbis and their disciples. The society nurtured and celebrated discipleship.[330]

---

[328] Louis Goldberg and Richard A. Robinson (editor), *God, Torah, Messiah: The Messianic Jewish Theology of Dr. Louis Goldberg* pp. 68-69.
[329] *Ibid.* pp. 17-18.
[330] David Bivin, *New Light on the Difficult Words of Jesus*, p. 11.

A sage (rabbi) who lived over one hundred years before Jesus is recorded to have said "Let your home be a meeting house for the sages, and cover yourself with the dust of their feet, and drink in their words thirstily."[331]

According to David Bivin, Jewish men were encouraged to give a part of their lives in following a sage. They could follow him intermittently, or they could follow them on a full time basis. If a married man wanted to follow a rabbi on a full time basis for more than thirty days, he could only do so with the permission of his wife. Amazingly, a disciple was expected to honor his rabbi above his own parents.[332]

> ➢ *Spiritual Friendships*

A disciple might bond to a particular rabbi, but he would often study under a variety of sages. Brad Young comments:

> Because a disciple should have broad knowledge, he would usually study with one rabbi for a number of years and then go study under another sage. The master teacher was a mentor whose purpose was to raise up disciples who would not only memorize his teachings but also live out the teachings in practical ways…The disciple walks with God by living out in practice the teaching of his rabbi.[333]

Since disciples would study with one another, they would have considered some fellow disciples *haverim* (friends). The term *haver* (singular) is defined as, "A student who

---

[331] *Ibid*, p. 12, quoted from *M. Avot* 1:4.
[332] *Ibid*, pp. 17-20. This may also explain Yeshua's words in Luke 14:26 (NASB), "If anyone comes to Me, and does not hate his own father and mother and wife and children and brothers and sisters, yes, and even his own life, he cannot be My disciple." The Hebrew idiom "hate" means to love less, to choose to please after another (that is, the disciple must put his rabbi – and for the believer, Jesus – above his own family when the two are in conflict).
[333] Brad H. Young, *Meet the Rabbis*, pp. 30-31.

partners with another in study to discuss a religious text and aid each other in learning. A female study partner is a *haverah*."[334] This concept could unlock the meaning of the term "friends" used of the early Christians, as seen in 3 John 1:15 (NIV), "Peace be to you. The *friends* greet you Greet the *friends* by name." The early believers were *haverim*!

> *Application of Discipleship to Messianics (Christians)*

Since Christian converts were called *talmidim* (disciples) before they were ever called "Christians" – as seen in Acts 6:7, for example – we can conclude that the early church embraced the Jewish concept of discipleship. To be a Christian thus included not only *belief* in Jesus as Messiah, but also *the desire to study*, learn, memorize, and develop friendships with fellow disciples. Thus the early church demonstrated that the purest Christianity is one absorbed with Bible study and relational involvement.

The rabbis later put it this way: "…two students who walk together without discussing the Torah deserve to be burned."[335]

In John 15:20a, Jesus says, "Remember the words I spoke to you…" This, in a nutshell, was the obsession of every true disciple within the Judaism of Yeshua's day.

Source Text for Yeshua's Midrashim About Discipleship

The Rabbis viewed the relationship of Elijah and Elisha as the ideal model of a rabbi and his disciples, as Spangler and Tverberg note.[336] This little fact opens the door to a proper

---

[334] Ann Spangler and Lois Tverberg, *Sitting At the Feet of Rabbi Jesus*, p. 227.
[335] *Sotah 49a.*

understanding of what discipleship *really* entails, especially when distilled and applied beyond the Jewish culture.

➤ *Yeshua and Elijah Correlated*

(I Kings 19:1-9, 15-16, Matthew 4:1-11)

The Gospel narratives seem to affirm that the ministry relationship between Elijah and Elisha was used as a model for the ministry of Messiah and his disciples. The theory passes the deductive check.

Even events within the life of Yeshua appear to follow the Elijah/Elisha pattern. Take Christ's preparation for ministry. Although Jesus' preparation for ministry and Elijah's preparation to anoint Elisha differ greatly, the similarities are worth consideration. I am assuming the reader is familiar with the Matthew 4:1-11 text (the temptation of Jesus in the wilderness), but let me present the correlated I Kings 19:5-9 text (NKJV):

> Then as he lay and slept under a broom tree, suddenly an angel touched him, and said to him, "Arise and eat." Then he looked, and there by his head was a cake baked on coals, and a jar of water. So he ate and drank, and lay down again. And the angel of the LORD came back the second time, and touched him, and said, "Arise and eat, because the journey is too great for you." So he arose, and ate and drank; and he went in the strength of that food forty days and forty nights as far as Horeb, the mountain of God.
>
> And there he went into a cave, and spent the night in that place; and behold, the word of the LORD came to him, and He said to him, "What are you doing here, Elijah?"

---

[336] "Where did the rabbis develop their ideas of discipleship? They found their model in Scripture, especially in the relationship of two men – the prophets Elijah and Elisha." The authors cite *Berakot 7a*. Spangler and Tverberg, pp. 54, 239.

Both Yeshua and Elijah were tempted in the wilderness. Elijah was tempted with despair (and succumbed to the temptation) while Messiah was tempted by the devil on three occasions (Matthew 4:1-11). Both seemingly fasted for forty days and nights without food or drink. In I Kings 8:8, God feeds Elijah with bread and water, and then Elijah travels for forty days until he reaches Horeb (Mount Sinai), presumably in Saudi Arabia.[337] There he meets with God and hears his voice. He also receives his directions from God.

Jesus' sequence was reversed. First, he is baptized by John and then tempted in the wilderness. At his baptism, he "meets" the Father and the Spirit. The Father speaks from heaven, and the Spirit anoints and empowers Yeshua for his ministry. Although not in exact sequence, the similarities in concept seem striking. His forty-day temptation in the wilderness was probably a time of waiting on the Father and being instructed about and prepared for his ministry via the Spirit.

The miracles Elijah and Elisha performed also presage Yeshua's miracles. Elijah's miracles recorded in I Kings include control of the weather (17:1) and resurrecting the dead (17:22). Elisha's miracles recorded in 2 Kings include resurrecting the dead (4:34), multiplying loaves of bread (4:42-44)[338], and healing a man plagued with leprosy (5:27).

---

[337] See *The Exodus Case* by Dr. Lennart Moller, pp. 267-277; see also Galatians 4:25.
[338] The ESV text reads, "A man came from Baal-shalishah, bringing the man of God bread of the firstfruits, twenty loaves of barley and fresh ears of grain in his sack. And Elisha said, 'Give to the men, that they may eat.' But his servant said, 'How can I set this before a hundred men?' So he repeated, 'Give them to the men,

> *Yeshua's Teachings About Discipleship: A Midrash on I Kings 19:19-21?*

I am convinced that Yeshua derived his basic teachings about discipleship from the Elijah and Elisha example. I am suggesting that these texts are correlated: I Kings 19:19-21,[339] Luke 9:57-62, Matthew 19:21, and Luke 5:27. These verses are quoted from the *New King James Version*:

I Kings 19:19-21

So he departed from there, and found Elisha the son of Shaphat, who was plowing with twelve yoke of oxen before him, and he was with the twelfth. Then Elijah passed by him and threw his mantle on him. And he left the oxen and ran after Elijah, and said, "Please let me kiss my father and my mother, and then I will follow you."

And he said to him, "Go back again, for what have I done to you?"

So Elisha turned back from him, and took a yoke of oxen and slaughtered them and boiled their flesh, using the oxen's equipment, and gave it to the people, and they ate. Then he arose and followed Elijah, and became his servant.

Luke 9:57-62:

Now it happened as they journeyed on the road, that someone said to Him, "Lord, I will follow You wherever You go." And Jesus said to him, "Foxes have holes and birds of the air have nests, but the Son of Man has nowhere to lay His head."

Then He said to another, "Follow Me." But he said, "Lord, let me first go and bury my father." Jesus said to him, "Let the dead bury their own dead, but you go and preach the kingdom of God."

And another also said, "Lord, I will follow You, but let me first go and bid them farewell who are at my house." But Jesus said to him, "No one, having put his hand to the plow, and looking back, is fit for the kingdom of God."

Matthew 19:21

---

that they may eat, for thus says the LORD, "They shall eat and have some left."' So he set it before them. And they ate and had some left, according to the word of the LORD" (2 Kings 4:42-44).

[339] I am grateful to Spangler and Tverberg for alerting me to the I Kings 19 text and its relevance to discipleship.

Jesus said to him, "If you want to be perfect, go, sell what you have and give to the poor, and you will have treasure in heaven; and come, follow Me."

Luke 5:27

After this, Jesus went out and saw a tax collector by the name of Levi sitting at his tax booth. "Follow me," Jesus said to him, and Levi got up, left everything and followed him.

> *Parallel Ideas*

Note how Elijah seems to appear abruptly to Elisha without formal notice. We can assume that Elijah and Elisha had experienced previous interaction. Elijah expects Elisha to drop whatever he is doing. When he requests to kiss his father and mother before he leaves to follow Elijah, it is difficult to interpret Elijah's response, "Go back again, for what have I done to you?" Perhaps the best interpretations are that either Elijah forbade Elisha from kissing his parents goodbye, or that he grudgingly allowed it.[340] When the text says, "So he went back…" we are told that he went back to slaughter the oxen. There is no actual mention of him returning to actually bid his parents farewell, so his going back may have been a return simply to "close shop."

In another vein, a simple "goodbye" kiss may not be what Elisha had in mind; he may have implied a traditional, lengthier delay, using the idea of "the kiss" as representative for the final act of departure. This compares amazingly with Yeshua's answer to the man who wanted to bury his dead father: "Let the dead bury their dead." In this instance, the

---

[340] Keil and Delitzsch comment, "The words 'what have I done to thee?' can only mean, I have not wanted to put any constraint upon thee, but leave it to they free will to decide in favour of the prophetic calling" (*Commentary on the Old Testament, Volume 3*, p. 261).

one-year period between initial burying and retrieving and sealing the bones in an ossuary is probably in mind.[341]

Elisha slaughtered his oxen and gave the meat to the people ("the poor"). He did not necessarily sell all his possessions, but disposed of whatever had to be *maintained* by him and thus might impede him from following Rabbi Elijah. In the Matthew 19:21 call to discipleship, Yeshua commanded the prospective disciple to sell all that he had (perhaps all that required attention?), thus removing all distractions. This passage (and others like it) is frequently misunderstood, in my opinion.

We must not confuse Yeshua's demand in this or related instances *as a permanent way of life* (as certain Monastic orders might), but *as a temporary relinquishment* while a disciple was pursuing a deeper relationship with God through following a rabbi *for a period*. The call to serve Jesus is a life-long call, but the call for *intense* spiritual training and indoctrination was a temporary call.[342] We might compare becoming a "disciple" to enrolling in a modern Bible college or seminary.

> *Yeshua's Teachings in Light of Hillel's precedent*

We can perhaps better understand Yeshua's call to discipleship by examining its similarities to those of Hillel:

---

[341] Michael L. Brown, *Answering Jewish Objections to Jesus*, Volume Four, p. 133. This is only one of his suggested interpretations, but one that seems evident to me.

[342] Some of the disciples were called in John 1, again in Mark 1 (and Matthew 4), and later – apparently to long-term discipleship – in Luke 5. It seems that they followed Christ off and on for two years, and then followed him on a full time basis for the last year or so of Yeshua's earthly ministry.

> He [Hillel] would stand at the gate of Jerusalem and meet people going to work. He questioned them, "How much will you make at work today?" One person would answer, "A denarius." Another replied, "Two denarii." Then he would ask them, "What will you do with your earnings?" They would reply, "We will buy what we need to live." Then he challenged them, "Why don't you come follow me and acquire knowledge of the Torah. Then you will receive life in this world as well as life in the future world?" In this way Hillel lived all his days and was able to bring many people under the wings of Heaven."[343]

If we compare Hillel's precedent with the teachings of Jesus, we would probably conclude that Yeshua's command in the instance cited above to "sell all that you have and give it to the poor" is primarily about removing hindrances from studying the Scriptures under a rabbi. Concern for the poor may be real, but it is clearly a secondary concern, a meaningful way to rid oneself of the strings that would hinder study. This has no relationship to socialism or any particular economic theory. The issue, rather, is that of priority.[344]

So much more to examine...

From 2 Kings 1:1-12, the passage in which Elijah discourages Elisha from following him before Elijah is swept up in a chariot, Yeshua may have derived the idea of making it *difficult* for potential disciples to follow him. Teachings like "counting the cost," "taking up the cross daily," etc. may have been either *Midrashim* or at least connected to this text.

---

[343] Avot R. Nat., vers. B, ch 26, quoted by Brad Young, *Meet the Rabbis*, pp. 191-192.
[344] Matthew 6:33 is clear: "But seek first his kingdom and his righteousness, and all these things will be given to you as well."

Other rabbis expressed the hardship involved with being either a rabbi or a disciple. As Bivin comments:

> The burden Jesus' disciples had to bear was a heavy one, but it was similar to what other first-century sages demanded of their disciples and would not have been considered extreme by the standards of first-century Jewish society.[345]

Elisha's relationship to Gehazi could be another area for inquiry if we chose to delve more deeply. Was the covetous Gehazi a Judas-like figure, a devil among us?[346] Did he personify the danger of covetousness, a danger that could completely neutralize the quest for godliness? Perhaps if Gehazi wanted to be great, he should have remained a "servant" to Elisha and become the servant of all.

Conclusion

Bible believing Christians need to rethink the subject of discipleship. Since the early believers were called "disciples," and since many of them did not physically leave their vocations to follow Jesus, we need to ask what discipleship means in the trans-cultural sense. I do not claim to have the complete answer, but I will assert that a disciple is one who desires to study, learn, and grow in the "grace and knowledge of our Lord Jesus

---

[345] Bivin, *New Light on the Difficult Words of Jesus*, p. 19.
[346] See 2 Kings 5:21-27, where Gehazi lies to take advantage of Naaman the Leper. Naaman had offered Elisha remuneration for his healing, but Elisha had refused. Gehazi feigned that Elisha had changed his mind, and he was there to collect.

Christ"[347] in concert with fellow *haverim*. Believers who have little desire to study are not disciples. And not all those who study are believers.

---

[347] 2 Peter 3:18 is perhaps the clearest distillation of the heart of Christian discipleship for all cultures and times.

Conclusion: My Hopes

We have examined a number of potential *Midrashim* in the ministry of Yeshua. Hopefully even the most skeptical reader is willing to concede that at least some of my suggested *Midrashim* are *Midrashim* indeed.

What are the implications of such a study, and where do I hope this will all lead? Optimist that I am, I hope big. Let me share seven hopes with you.

First, I hope that Christians will return to the Jewish Roots of our faith as a way to better understand Yeshua and the *Second Testament*. This includes learning from Messianic Judaism and embracing the truth that our Sovereign God has determined to frame our faith – past, present, and future – within the Jewish context. Perhaps some will embrace the idea that Christianity is a form of Judaism, as I have.

If we can rid ourselves of the vestiges of anti-Semitism, we may sharpen our understanding of Scripture. We would also experience a renewed interest in the relevance of the *First Testament*, believing once again that not only are all Scriptures inspired, but also that all are "profitable…"[348] Many Christians do not believe that the *First Testament* is profitable or useful for doctrine.

Second, I hope evangelicalism will return to Scripture absorption. If the *First Testament* is the Older Testament but not the Obsolete Testament,[349] perhaps we will recognize the value of a Psalm 1 or a Psalm 119 faith.

In a day in which music and self-help sermons have largely replaced the in-depth teaching of the Word, we need a call to a faith that will not displace the primacy of God's Word. Study, of course, must result in obedience, which will result in other forms of worship. But study is not just a means to obedience: God is glorified when we absorb ourselves in his Word. The process matters as much as the result. We exist to glorify

---

[348] See 2 Timothy 3:16-17, and notice how the term "all" applies to more than "inspired," but to the entire list of terms.

[349] There are aspects of the First Covenant which have become obsolete, but that is a complicated discussion. Let me say briefly that the differences between the Covenants are not primarily about specific regulations. The First Covenant is one in which few participants are regenerate, but the Second Covenant includes ONLY the regenerate.

God, not primarily to make this world a better place. But if we glorify God and obey him, we will make this world a better place as a result of our obedience.

Third, I also hope that we will learn about the dangers of tradition, religion, and a faith that does not return directly to the Scriptures as we observe the errors of Rabbinic Judaism. We need to be careful not to displace a relationship with God, mediated through his Son, nurtured by his Word, and animated by his Spirit. Replacing the Word with religion, rituals, artwork, music, drama, and "spirituality" –or accumulated traditions – is the temptation of fallen man. Using Scripture as just another "element of worship" creates a façade. We are to pour over, read and re-read, meditate upon, study, debate, and memorize God's Word.

My **fourth** hope applies to those seeking to interpret and exegete Scripture. I hope that interpreters begin to see the minimal value of studying the church past her first three or four centuries as a source of doctrinal determination. We would be better served to channel our attentions toward understanding the background of first century Christianity, the Jewish background. Jesus did not teach in light of Nicaea or the Westminster Confession, for example; but he did teach in light of Hillel. Paul taught gentiles, but he taught them much like Jewish rabbis taught God-fearing gentiles. His foundation was not the Roman or Greek culture, but his assumptions are also Jewish.

If we want to return to the original intent of the *Second Testament* authors, why would we focus upon the accumulated teaching of gentile believers detached from the early church by hundreds of years, often characterized by an anti-Semitic stance that soured them toward the Jewish culture? It was that Jewish culture that produced the original church. This negative bias significantly affected Christian hermeneutics.

I am not saying that later believers could not (and did not) make valuable observations about the Scriptures or provide some valuable perspectives. I am not saying it is wrong to study church history, or that we need no academics in this field. I am suggesting that our focus should be upon the intended meaning of the New Testament authors. From an interpretative viewpoint, we have been looking in the wrong places.

Fifth, I also hope that pastors and teachers will return to Biblical exposition. Let me share some flashbacks about my interest in the *Midrash*. The second of these two involves the subject of expository preaching.

In a sense, my quest for *Midrash* began before I knew it began. My burning desire, as a young man of twenty, was to really understand some of the radical teachings of the

Sermon on the Mount. I knew the apparent meaning was not quite right, and I felt that attempts to exegete it were dubious. Even then I recognized the folly of substituting application for interpretation, or viewing truth as the averaging of two apparently extreme (but conflicting) passages.

The more current impetus came when a popular preacher asserted, "Jesus did not preach expository sermons." As I thought about that statement, I wondered. I asked myself, "What if Jesus did preach expository sermons, and we have failed to pick it up?" I have obviously concluded that this is exactly what happened.

I love expository preaching – and the results I see from it. Topical preaching has its place, but Christians really do need the whole counsel of God, some of which is not very trendy or seemingly relevant. This challenge motivated me.

Expository preaching, however, needs to heed the lesson of this book. Passages should be studied in couplets, when possible. For example, I am currently preaching through Numbers and find myself in chapter 14:1-25. By way of application, I am taking the congregation to the *Second Testament Midrash* on this event, Hebrews 3:1-19. When addressing Numbers 14:26-44, I will take them to its *Second Testament Midrash,* the famous Hebrews 6:4-6. If I were to preach on Philippians 2:9-11, I would bring up the mother text, Isaiah 45:23.

My **sixth** hope is this: Perhaps we can forsake the aura and theological dignity of an ancient but (initially) anti-Semitic viewpoint that God is done with Israel forever. Instead, we need to return to a theology and a hermeneutical viewpoint in which the *Second Testament* is built upon the *First Testament*, one in which the Second Testament is a SLIGHT MODIFICATION over the First, but appears more distinct than it is because it is primarily addressing God-fearing gentiles who are under the wings of Israel.

Although gentiles are nowhere called to relate to God under the Mosaic Covenant, the theology of the Second Covenant (including eschatology) is not radical replacement of the First, but refinement and detail. Thus we learn in the First Testament that God will one day set up his Kingdom on the earth, but the Second Testament specifies its duration (1,000 years). We have lost nothing major from the First to Second Testament; we have merely gained some previous unrevealed truths. Thus, eschatologically speaking, we can "build our charts" from the First Testament, then add details and refinements from the Second.

This is also true (or should be) in other areas of theology. For example, the foundation of our understanding of God is based upon the Unity and Oneness of God as presented in the Torah. That God is Three Persons can be surmised in retrospect within the *Tannakh*, but it is more so a Second Testament refinement,[350] one which does not negate the Torah's teaching of One United God. Thus we would consider God's unity as the more foundational concept upon which we must build.

Since **seven** is the "perfect number," my last hope is that this book will serve as an impetus for further research, study and refinement about Yeshua's use of *Midrash* and how this affects our understanding of his life, his words, and his church.

To him be the praise and glory, both now and forever, Amen.

---

[350] Matthew 28:19-20 is still the best verse to define the Trinity. The Trinity can be thought of as the complete summation of all Bible teaching about God's unity and God as three distinct Persons.

Glossary of Terms and Abbreviations

Bet Hillel: "The House of Hillel," one of the two divisions of the Pharisees. In Jesus' day, a minority of the rabbis identified with *Bet Hillel*. Hillel ministered between 30 B.C. up until his death in 10 A.D. Hillel promoted a humanitarian interpretation of the Torah and held that gentiles could be saved without becoming full converts to Judaism. After Jerusalem was destroyed (70A.D.) *Bet Hillel* became the predominant form of Judaism.

Bet Shammai: "The House of Shammai," the other main division of the Pharisees. The majority of the rabbis in Jesus' day were aligned with *Bet Shammai*. Shammai lived from 50 B.C. to 30 A.D. Shammai was noted for his harsh, strict, and separatist interpretations. *Bet Shammai's* viewpoints wielded more influence during Jesus' time than *Hillel's*. After the destruction of Jerusalem and a later revolt, *Bet Shammai's* influence soon died out.

Essenes: Also known as "The Dead Sea Scroll People" or "Qumran Community." This group was a reactionary movement of devout Jews who felt that mainstream Judaism had been compromised. Some suggest this group was loosely connected with *Bet Hillel*.

First Testament: A preferred way to refer to the Old Testament.

HaShem: "The Name," a term used by Jews for God to avoid pronouncing "Yahweh" or "Adonai," for fear that they might violate the commandment not to misuse God's Name.

Hasidim (pl): In ancient times, the term was used of pious Jews, holy men who sought to go beyond Torah requirements. The modern *Hasidic* Jews derive their name from this term, although they tend more toward the emotional and mystical aspects of Judaism.

Haver, Haverim (Pl): A "friend" who became a "study buddy" and accountability partner in the study and practice of Torah.

Karaite: A relatively modern sect of Jews who seek to live in obedience to the Torah and First Testament, but who reject the Oral Law (as recorded in the Talmud) as binding. Some propose that Jesus was an early version of a Karaite.

Kosher: Ritually clean for Jewish use; the term often refers to food, but it used of other restricted items as well.

Messianic, Messianic Jew: A believer in Jesus with a Jewish background who wishes to continue identifying with his Jewish heritage.

***Midrash, Midrashim* (Pl):** A teaching. As used in *this* book, a teaching that is a *Second Testament* interpretation or application of a *First Testament* text. *Midrash* later came to refer to a non-literal method of interpretation (or a collection of sermons), but that is not how we use the term.

***Mishnah*:** The oldest part of the *Talmud* and the foundation of the Oral Law. Although written down in about 200 A.D., its memorized teachings extend back to 200 B.C.

***Mitzvah, mitzvot* (Pl):** A commandment, an opportunity to obey God. The Torah contains 613 *mitzvot*.

***Pesha, Peshat* (Pl):** Normal, straightforward interpretation.

Pharisee: A separatist group of Jews who sought to maintain an uncorrupted form of Judaism – in theory. Begun by Ezra, all the Pharisees shared certain common beliefs, but many Pharisees had lost the original vision of the movement. Most of the beliefs of Jesus and the early church reflect the Pharisaical belief system. Their main competitors were the Sadducees. Modern Judaism has descended from the Pharisees' belief system.

Rabbi: Teacher. An expert in the Old Testament Law who sought to influence others. Notable teachers were originally called sages, but the term "sage" eventually gave way to the term "rabbi." Modern rabbis only bear some similarity to their ancient counterparts.

Regenerate: Born again, brought to spiritual life. In the New Testament, repentance and faith in Jesus Christ evidence that the Holy Spirit has regenerated a person.

Sadducee: A liberal Jewish sect, descended from Zadok the priest. The Sadducees originally embraced mainstream Jewish beliefs, but by Jesus' day had embraced a liberal form of Judaism; they denied the First Testament except for the Torah. They denied the reality of angels and the after life. The high priestly family and their rich associates were Sadducees. After Jerusalem's destruction in 70 A.D., the Sadducees ceased to exist.

Sage: Teacher. The ancient term for a rabbi.

Scribe: Scribes were often also rabbis. Although some copied Scripture (hence their name), they were experts in the Torah.

Second Testament: A preferred way to refer to the New Testament.

Septuagint (LXX): The Greek translation of the Hebrew Scriptures.

Shema (also Sh'ma): The recitation of Deuteronomy 6:4-9, 11:13-21, and Numbers 15:37-41 as a prayer. Devout Jews recite the Shema daily. It is an important part of a synagogue service, and considered the pillar of Jewish belief.

SOM: Sermon on the Mount (an abbreviation).

Synoptic Gospels, Synoptics: Matthew, Mark, and Luke. These are seen with the "same eye" and thus bear a lot of similarity.

Talmid, talmidim **(Pl):** Disciple, disciples.

Talmud: The written version of the oral Jewish Law taught by the notable sages from 200 B.C. to about 500 A.D. The Talmud is a massive work. The oldest part of the Talmud is the *Mishnah*.

Tanakh (Tannakh, Tanach): The Old Testament (*First Testament*). It can be spelled a variety of ways, and is an invented, composite word consisting of syllables from the Hebrew words for the Law, the Prophets, and the Writings.

Targum: A paraphrase that interprets and adds to the written text of the Tanakh, usually composed in Aramaic.

Torah: Instruction, Law. The Five Books of Moses (The Pentateuch) are typically referred to as The Torah.

Yahweh: God's personal name, meaning the "self-existent one." It is typically translated as LORD in the First Testament.

Yeshua: Jesus. This is his Hebrew name, and it means, "Yahweh is Salvation." This is a variant on the name Joshua, and was a common name in first century Israel.

Yom Kippur: The Day of Atonement.

Zealots: A Jewish terrorist group, seeking to undermine Roman rule.

Bibliography

Anderson, R.T. "Samaritans." *The International Standard Bible Encyclopedia, Volume Four*. Grand Rapids: Eerdmans, 1988.

"Athronges." *Wikipedia*. 19 May 2010. <http://en.wikipedia.org/wiki/Athronges>.

Benware, Paul. Class Lecture. *The Synoptic Gospels*. Moody Bible Institute, Chicago, IL. Spring, 1978.

Bivin, David. *New Light on the Difficult Words of Jesus: Insights from His Jewish Context*. Holland, MI: En-Gedi Resource Center, 2005.

——————— "Online Glossary." *Jerusalem Perspective*. 19 January 2010 < www.jerusalemperspective.com>.

Bivin, David, and Roy Blizzard. *Understanding the Difficult Words of Jesus*. Aracadia: Makor Foundation, 1983.

Bronner, Ethan, "Ancient Tablet Ignites Debate on Messiah and Resurrection." *New York Times* (online), July 6, 2008. 20 May 2010. <http://www.nytimes.com/2008/07/06/world/middleeast/06stone.html?_r=3&oref=slogin&oref=slogin>.

Brenton, Sir Lancelot C.L. *The Septuagint with Apocrypha: Greek and English*. Peabody, MA: Hendrickson, 1986 printing.

Bromiley, Geoffrey W. *The International Standard Bible Encyclopedia (Four Volumes)*. Grand Rapids, MI: Eerdmans, 1979.

Brown, Colin (editor). *The New International Dictionary of New Testament Theology (Four Volume Set)*. Grand Rapids, MI: Regency/Zondervan, 1986.

Brown, Michael L. *Answering Jewish Objections to Jesus, Volume One: General and Historical Objections*. Grand Rapids, MI: Baker Books, 2000.

———————-. *Answering Jewish Objections to Jesus, Volume Two: Theological Objections*. Grand Rapids, MI: Baker Books, 2000.

―――――――――. *Answering Jewish Objections to Jesus, Volume Three: Messianic Prophecy Objections*. Grand Rapids, MI: Baker Books, 2003.

―――――――――. *Answering Jewish Objections to Jesus, Volume Four: New Testament Objections*. Grand Rapids, MI: Baker Books, 2007.

―――――――――. *Answering Jewish Objections to Jesus, Volume Five: Traditional Jewish Objections*. San Francisco: Purple Pomegranate, 2009.

Bruce, F.F. *The Canon of Scripture*. Downers Grove, IL: InterVarsity Press, 1988.

Carson, D.A. *The Sermon on the Mount*. Grand Rapids, MI: Baker, 1978.

Carson, D.A.; O'Brien, Peter T.; and Seifred, Mark A. (editors). *Justification and Variegated Nomism, Volume One: The Complexities of Second Temple Judaism*. Tubingen: Mohr Siebeck; Grand Rapids, MI: Baker Academic, 2001.

―――――――――――――――――――――――――――――. *Justification and Variegated Nomism, Volume Two: The Paradoxes of Paul*. Tubingen: Mohr Siebeck; Grand Rapids, MI: Baker Academic, 2004.

Chafer, Lewis Sperry. *Grace*. Philadelphia: The Sunday School Times Company, 1922.

Cowley, A., Jacobs, Joseph, and Huxley, Henry Minor. "Samaritans." *The Jewish Encyclopedia*. 10 May 2010. <http://www.jewishencyclopedia.com/view.jsp?artid=110&letter=S&search=Samaritans>.

Craigie, P.C. *The Book of Deuteronomy (New International Commentary on the Old Testament)*. Grand Rapids: Eerdmans, 1976.

Daniel, Orville E. *A Harmony of the Four Gospels, Second Edition*. Grand Rapids, MI: Baker, 1996.

Daube, David. *The New Testament and Rabbinic Judaism*. Reprint. Peabody, MA: Hendrickson [1956], 1994.

"Direct Realism." *Wikipedia*. 10 June 2010 <http://en.wikipedia.org/wiki/Directrealism>

Etshalom, Yitzchak. "Parashat Mishpatim," *Torah.org*. 22 June 2010.
<http://www.torah.org/advanced/mikra/5757/sh/dt.57.2.06.html>

Falk, Harvey. *Jesus the Pharisee*. Eugene, Oregon: Wipf and Stock Publishers, 1985.

Finkel, Avraham Yaakov, *The Torah Revealed*. San Francisco: Josey-Bass, 2004.

Fischer, John (editor). *The Enduring Paradox*. Baltimore: Lederer/Messianic Jewish Publishers, 2000.

Flusser, David. *Judaism and the Origins of Christianity*. Jerusalem: Magnes Press, 1989.

Friedman, David. *They Loved the Torah*. Baltimore: Lederer Books/Messianic Jewish Publishers, 2001.

Fruchtenbaum, Arnold G. *Israelology: The Missing Link in Systematic Theology*. Tustin, CA: Ariel Ministries, 1992 revision.

Gill, John. *John Gill's Exposition of the Bible*. Bible Study Tools. 10 May 2010. http://www.biblestudytools.com/commentaries/gills-exposition-of-the-bible/matthew-5-22.html.

Gill, John. *John Gill's Exposition of the Bible*. Studylight.org. 22 May 2010.
<http://www.studylight.org/com/geb/view.cgi?book=joh&chapter=001&verse=021>.

Girdlestone, Robert B. *Synonyms of the Old Testament*. Grand Rapids, MI: Eerdmans, 1987 (reprint).

Goodrick, Edward W., and Kohlenberger, John R. III. *The NIV Exhaustive Concordance*. Grand Rapids, MI: Zondervan, 1990.

Goldberg, Louis. *God, Torah, Messiah: The Messianic Theology of Dr. Louis Goldberg*. San Francisco. Purple Pomegranate Productions, 2009.

Gordon, Nehemia. *The Hebrew Yeshua Vs. the Greek Jesus*. no city: Hilkiah Press, 2006.

Greenlee, J. Harold. *Introduction to New Testament Textual Criticism*. Grand Rapids, MI: Eerdmans, [1964] 1977.

Greenstone, Julius H. "Prosbul." *The Jewish Encyclopedia*. 22 December 2009. < http://www.jewishencyclopedia.com/view.jsp?artid=555&letter=P&search=prosbul>.

Grudem, Wayne. *Systematic Theology: An Introduction to Biblical Doctrine*. Leicester: Inter-Varsity Press; Grand Rapids, MI: Zondervan, 1994.

Hamilton, James M. "Were Old Covenant Believers Indwelt by the Holy Spirit?" *Themelios 30* (2004), 12-22. *Southern Baptist Theological Seminary*. June, 2008. 3 July 2010. <http://jimhamilton.files.wordpress.com/2008/06/them30-1.pdf>.

Harris, R. Laird; Archer, Gleason L., and Waltke, Bruce K. *Theological Wordbook of the Old Testament (2 Volumes)*. Chicago: Moody Press, 1980.

Heschel, Abraham J. *The Prophets*. Peabody, MA: Pinch Press, 1962.

Hislop, Alexander. *The Two Babylons or The Papal Worship*. Neptune, NJ: Loizeaux Brothers, 1959 (reprint).

Hoehner, Harold W. *Chronological Aspects of the Life of Christ*. Grand Rapids, MI: Academie/Zondervan, 1977.

_____. "Herod." *The International Standard Bible Encyclopedia, Volume Two*. Grand Rapids: Eerdmans, 1988.

"Inspiration." *Jewish Encyclopedia*. 11 November 2009 <http://www.jewishencyclopedia.com/view.jsp?artid=152&letter=I&search=inspiration >.

Jacobs, Joseph and Blau, Ludwig. "Torah." *The Jewish Encyclopedia*. 15 March 2009. < http://www.jewishencyclopedia.com/view.jsp?artid=265&letter=T&search=Torah>.

Jacobs, Joseph and Horovitz, S. "Midrash." *The Jewish Encyclopedia*. 11 November 2009. <www.jewishencyclopedia.com/ view.jsp?artid=586&letter=M&search=Midrash>.

Jacobson, Simon. *Toward a Meaningful Life with Simon Jacobson*. Radio Show Transcript, May 21, 2000. 10 June 2010 < www.meaningfullife.com/personal/emotions/Humor.php>.

Jastrow, Marcus and Mendelsohn, S. "Bet Hillel and Bet Shammai," *The Jewish Encylopedia.* 24 June 2010 http://www.jewishencyclopedia.com/view.jsp?artid= 956&letter=B&search=Bet%20Hillel>.

"Just Don't Call Me Late for Supper: The Parable of the Great Supper." *Parables and Paradise: Living the Paradoxes of Faith.* 28 June 2010 <http://www.crossmarks.com/parable/5supper.htm>.

Kaiser, Walter C. Jr. *Toward An Exegetical Theology.* Grand Rapids, MI: Baker, 1981.

"Karaite Judaism." *Wikipedia.* 25 May 2010 < http://en.wikipedia.org/wiki/Karaite_Judaism>.

Keil, C.F., and Delitzsch, F. *Commentary on the Old Testament in Ten Volumes, Volume III.* Grand Rapids, MI: Eerdmans, no date.

Kinzer, Mark S. *Post-Missionary Messianic Judaism.* Grand Rapids, MI: Brazos Press, 2005.

Kitchen, K.A. *On the Reliability of the Old Testament.* Grand Rapids, MI: Zondervan, 2003.

Kohler, Kaufmann and Schreiber, E. "Humility." *The Jewish Encyclopedia.* 28 June 2010. < http://www.jewishencyclopedia.com/view.jsp?artid=962&letter=H&search= Humility>.

Kohn, Daniel. "Brit Milah: Rabbinic Interpretations." *My Jewish Learning.* 28 June 2010 <http://www.myjewishlearning.com/life/Life_Events/Newborn_Ceremonies/History_and_Themes/Ceremonies_for_Boys/History/Rabbinic_Understandings.shtml>.

Lamsa, George M. *The Holy Bible from Ancient Eastern Manuscripts.* Philadelphia: A. J. Holman, 1957.

"The Law of Moses is Eternal." *HaDavar Messianic Ministries.* 3 June 2010 <http://hadavar.org/drupal/content/law-moses-eternal>.

Lee, Richard. *The Teaching of Jesus from Deuteronomy*, East Midlands School of Ministry. 2006. 6 November 2009 <http://www.schoolofministry.org.uk/Admin/Content/Resources/Teaching%20of%20Jesus%20from%20Deuteronomy.pdf>.

Lieber, David L. (senior editor). *Etz Hayim: Torah and Commentary.* New York: The Rabbinical Assembly (The United Synagogue of Conservative Judaism), 2004.

Lindsey, Robert. "The Kingdom Of God: God's Power Among Believers." *The Jerusalem Perspective.* January 1, 2004. 10 June 2010 < http://jerusalemperspective.com>.

Lightfoot, John. *A Commentary on the New Testament from the Talmud and Hebraica, (Four Volume Set).* no city: Hendrickson, [1658] 1995 (reprint).

Longenecker, Richard N. *Biblical Exegesis in the Apostolic Period.* Grand Rapids, MI: Eerdmans, 1999.

MacArthur, John F. *The Gospel According to Jesus.* Grand Rapids, MI: Academie/Zondervan, 1988.

Moller, Lennart. *The Exodus Case: New Discoveries Confirm the Historical Exodus.* Copenhagen: Scandinavia Publishing, 2002.

Morris, Leon. *Testaments of Love.* Grand Rapids, MI: Eerdmans, 1981.

Moseley, Ron. *Yeshua: A Guide to the Real Jesus and the Original Church.* Baltimore: Lederer/Messianic Jewish Publishers, 1996.

Neusner, Jacob. *A Midrash Reader.* Minneapolis. Fortress Press, 1990.

——————. *Judaism in the Beginning of Christianity.* Philadelphia. Fortress Press, 1984.

Pentecost, J. Dwight. *The Words and Works of Jesus Christ.* Grand Rapids, MI: Acadamie/Zondervan, 1981.

Pryor, Keren Hannah. "Emor 'Say,'10 May 2008." *A Taste of Torah*" (Daily Messianic Email Devotional). Center for Judaic-Christian Studies. www.jcstudies.com.

Punton, Anne. *The World Jesus Knew: Beliefs and Customs from the Time of Jesus.* Grand Rapids, MI: Monarch Books, 1996.

Rausch, David A. *Building Bridges: Understanding Jews and Judaism*. Chicago: Moody Press, 1988.

"The Rebbe Speaks on the Noahide." *Noahide.org*. 24 June 2010. http://www.noahide.org/article.asp?Level=351&Parent=90>

Restak, Richard. *The New Brain: How the Modern Age is Rewiring Your Mind*. no city: Rodale, 2003.

Rienicker, Fritz. *A Linguistic Key to the Greek New Testament*. Grand Rapids, MI: Regency/Zondervan, 1980.

Robertson, A.T. *A Harmony of the Gospels For Students of the Life of Christ: Based on the Broadus Harmony in the Revised Version*. New York: Harper and Row, 1950.

Safrai, Shmuel, "Jesus and the Hasidim." *The Jerusalem Perspective*. January 1, 2004; revised December 17, 2008. 10 June 2010 < http://www.jerusalemperspective.com>.

Sacks, Stuart. *Hebrews Through A Hebrew's Eyes*. Baltimore: Lederer/Messianic Jewish, 1995.

Sanders, E.P. *Jesus and Judaism*. London: SCM, 1985.

Schneider, Bernard N. *Deuteronomy: A Favored Book of Jesus*. Winona Lake, IN: BMH Books, 1970.

Schurer, Emil. *A History of the Jewish People in the Time of Jesus Christ, Volume I*. no city: Hendrickson, 2008 (reprint).

Spangler, Ann and Tverberg, Lois. *Sitting At the Feet of Rabbi Jesus: How the Jewishness of Jesus Can Transform Your Faith*. Grand Rapids, MI: Zondervan, 2009.

Steinsaltz, Adin. *The Essential Talmud*. no city: Basic Books, 1976.

Stern, David H. *Jewish New Testament Commentary*. Clarksville, MD: Jewish New Testament Publications, 1992.

_____. *Restoring the Jewishness of the Gospel*. Clarksville, MD: Jewish New Testament Publications, 1990.

The Talmud (Socino Edition). Come and Hear. <http://www.come-and-hear.com/talmud/>.

Tigay, Jeffrey, "Deuteronomy." *My Jewish Learning.* 28 June 2010 <http://www.myjewishlearning.com/texts/Bible/Torah/Deuteronomy.shtml>.

VanderLugt, Herbert. "The Good Atheist" from *Our Daily Bread.* Radio Bible Class. November 6, 2005. 17 February 2010. <http://odb.org/2004/11/06/the-good-atheist/>.

Varner, William C. "Jesus and the Pharisees: A Jewish Perspective" *Personal Freedom Outreach,* 1996. 18 November 2009 < http://www.pfo.org/pharisee.htm>.

Wallace, Daniel. "Is Intra-Canonical Theological Development Compatible with a High Bibliology?" *Bible.org*: Delivered at the Evangelical Theological Society Southwestern Regional Meeting, Criswell College, March 1, 2002. 5 July 2010 <http://bible.org/article/intra-canonical-theological-development-compatible-high-bibliology>.

Werblowsky, R. J. Zwi, and Wigoder, Geoffrey (editors). *The Encyclopedia of the Jewish Religion.* New York: Holt, Rinehart and Winston, Inc., 1965.

Witherington, Ben III. *The Acts of the Apostles.* Grand Rapids, MI: Eerdmans, 1998.

Wordbase Greek, 02 March 2010. <http://greek.kihlman.eu/>.

Young, Brad H. *Jesus the Jewish Theologian.* Peabody, MA: Hendrickson, 1995.

——————. *Meet the Rabbis.* Peabody, MA: Hendrickson, 2007.

About the Author....

Edward J. Vasicek was born and reared in the Chicago area and reached through the ministry of Cicero Bible Church. He graduated from Moody Bible Institute with highest honors in 1979, receiving a B.A. in Pastoral/Greek. Ed did additional graduate work through San Diego Bible College and Seminary.

"Pastor Ed" has served as the pastor of Highland Park Church in Kokomo, Indiana, since 1983. He and his wife, Marylu, will be celebrating 30 years of marriage and are the proud parents of two adult children.

Ed began delving into Jewish Roots studies in the early 1990's, and has been an occasional guest speaker at the Messianic Congregation, *Ahavot Yeshua*, in Indianapolis. In addition, Ed has addressed the *Student Theological Society* of the Moody Bible Institute regarding the use of *Midrash* in the New Testament. He has nicknamed himself, "The Midrash Detective."

Ed's writing experience is significant. Since 1999, he has authored a weekly "Opinion Page" column for the daily community newspaper, *The Kokomo Tribune*; he has published more than 500 editorial columns, and has been quoted in papers around the nation, including *USA Today*. Ed has published articles in *Pulpit Helps Magazine*, *The Sharper Iron* website, and some of his papers are posted throughout the web on theological and seminary websites.

Ed invites you to read his articles via the church website, **www.highlandpc.com**.

You may contact Ed by email at <edvasicek@gmail.com>.

Watch for "The Midrash Key Discussion and Teacher's Guide for Group Study."

Printed in Great Britain
by Amazon.co.uk, Ltd.,
Marston Gate.